USING ENGLISH
GRAMMAR AND WRITING SKILLS

FIRST COURSE

ADRIAN B. SANFORD

◁ CENTER FOR THE STUDY OF INSTRUCTION
San Francisco

HBJ HARCOURT BRACE JOVANOVICH
New York   Chicago   San Francisco   Atlanta   Dallas   *and*   London

THE AUTHOR

ADRIAN B. SANFORD has taught English for more than a quarter of a century. He has also written materials for English instruction and conducted workshops for educators.

CONSULTING EDUCATORS AND TEACHERS

ENNO KLAMMER
Eastern Oregon State College
La Grande, Oregon

CYNTHIA BAKER
Starr King Intermediate
Carmichael, California

MARIAN O. JENKINS
Coral Springs High School
Coral Springs, Florida

JACK STRANGE
Arcade Intermediate
Carmichael, California

JO ANN STEWART
Lowell High School
San Francisco, California

BARBARA S. DEAN
Will Rogers School
Fair Oaks, California

ROBERT LEON
Palo Alto High School
Palo Alto, California

SYBILLE IRWIN
Winston Churchill Intermediate
Carmichael, California

KEITH CALDWELL
Kennedy High School
Fremont, California

JUDY A. KANTER
Howe Avenue Intermediate
Sacramento, California

KEITH WILL
San Juan Unified School District
Carmichael, California

BARBARA COULTER
Louis Pasteur School
Orangeville, California

ACKNOWLEDGEMENTS

The publisher gratefully acknowledges the contributions of Jo Ann Stewart and Charlotte Herbert to the preparation of the Review Exercises for the series.

For permission to reprint copyrighted material, grateful acknowledgment is made to the following sources:

Harcourt Brace Jovanovich, Inc.: Excerpts from *The HBJ School Dictionary.* Copyright © 1977 by Harcourt Brace Jovanovich, Inc.

The H.W. Wilson Company: Excerpt from *Readers' Guide to Periodical Literature.* Copyright © 1977 by The H.W. Wilson Company.

DIANA WHITELEY
Project Editor

PATRICIA HOSLEY
Editor

SALLY THOMPSON
Text Designer

Printed in the United States of America

ISBN 0-15-311700-1

TO THE STUDENT

As you begin using this book, take time to become familiar with its special features. Notice the organization of sections and chapters of the book as shown in the Contents. Look within a chapter to see how the rules and definitions are printed. Note the use of color and special type to highlight important points.

An alphabetized index in the back of the book lists all the important topics in the textbook, with their page numbers. The colored tabs at the corners of the pages allow you to find any topic by its chapter number. The glossary in the back of the book gives an alphabetical listing of special terms in English. Each is followed by a definition. Many of the terms have examples to illustrate their meaning or use.

On certain pages you can see cross references printed in the margins. These refer you to other parts of the text where you can find additional information.

These features—and more—have been built into the book to aid you.

From this textbook you can learn a great deal about how to improve your use of English. Improvement, however, requires that you apply yourself to studying the book and to using what you can learn from it. As either a textbook assigned by your teacher or a reference tool in which you find what you need, this book offers you the opportunity to grow stronger in using English.

A.B.S.

CONTENTS

UNIT FOUR: MECHANICS

UNIT FIVE: AIDS AND
ENRICHMENT

UNIT ONE

GRAMMAR AND STRUCTURE

Parts of Speech
Phrases
Sentences

1

PARTS OF SPEECH

Nouns, Pronouns, Adjectives

Every word you write or speak is a *part of speech* with its own special name and use. Some words stand for things you can see or think about. Other words tell about actions. Still other words describe someone or something. The eight parts of speech are *nouns, pronouns, adjectives, verbs, adverbs, conjunctions, prepositions,* and *interjections.* You will study them in the first two chapters of this textbook.

NOUNS

1a A noun is a word or a group of words used to name someone or something.

A noun may name a living thing.

EXAMPLES   humans, animals, insects, plants,
girl, boy, father, mother, doctors,
goats, Mr. Cross, Ms. Gomez, tree,
fleas, wolf, fish, donkey, Rin Tin
Tin, glider

A noun may name a nonliving thing.

EXAMPLES   house, mountains, roof, footballs,
tables, car, Empire State Building,
movies, checkers, candle,
television, ice, *Mad* (magazine),
golf, shadows

A noun may name a place.

EXAMPLES   beach, Portland, Central Park,
Hawaii, Paris, home, zoo, Pacific
Ocean, Japan, Disney World

A noun may name an action.

EXAMPLES   running, exercise, laughing,
laughter, fights, debate, struggle,
teasing, climbing, dancing

A noun may name an idea, a season, or a period of
time.

EXAMPLES   love, hate, freedom, happiness,
spring, winter, midnight, 6:00,
morning, January, afternoon,
lifetime

A noun may name a quantity or measurement.

EXAMPLES   yard, ton, kilogram, meter, bushel,
minute

Any group of words used to name someone or something is a noun.

EXERCISE 1 Number your paper from 1 to 10. After each number write the nouns that appear in each sentence.

EXAMPLE Thoroughbreds are horses that are used in racing.

Thoroughbreds, horses, racing

1. Pt. Reyes National Seashore is located about fifty miles north of San Francisco, California.
2. The park consists of many acres on a broad peninsula next to the Pacific Ocean.
3. Hikers and campers can find hills, meadows, streams, and beaches there.
4. Morgan horses are raised at the headquarters of the park.
5. White deer roam the foggy land.
6. Whales may be seen from the bluff above Drake's Bay.
7. Many historians believe Sir Francis Drake landed on the peninsula when he was sailing the Pacific for Queen Elizabeth.
8. In the past, dairying was an important business at Pt. Reyes.
9. The stagecoach used to stop at the little town of Olema.
10. Now a restaurant there serves the best biscuits and honey in California.

Nouns are of two kinds: *proper nouns* and *common nouns.*

Proper Nouns

(1) A proper noun names a particular person, place, group, or thing.

EXAMPLES Juan, Ellen, Marcia Blum, Dr. Ellis,
              King Kong, Bay City Ramblers,
              St. Louis, Columbia River,
              Washington Monument, Viking I

EXERCISE 2 Read the following sentences. Then number a sheet of paper from 1 to 5. List the proper nouns in each sentence.

EXAMPLE Viking II was scheduled to land on
             Mars on Thursday.

Viking II, Mars, Thursday

1. When we were in Cincinnati, we watched the Reds play the Dodgers at Riverfront Stadium.
2. We also saw the Ohio River that flows between Ohio and Kentucky.
3. Early frontier explorers like Daniel Boone traveled on the river.
4. On our way back to Seattle, we visited the Falling Stone Silver Mine on the Dry Gulch River just outside the city of Rich Vein.
5. That's where my brother Mickey got sick from washing down two hamburgers with almost a quart of orange juice.

EXERCISE 3 Write these four headings on a sheet of paper: *People, Groups, Places, Things.* List at least ten proper nouns under each heading.

EXAMPLES   PEOPLE   GROUPS

Elsa Jones   *Scouts*
Tom Smith   *Dodgers*

            PLACES   THINGS

Washington   *Viking I*
Phoenix   *Datsun*

Hint: A proper noun always begins with   See Capitali-
a capital letter.   zation, p. 173

Common Nouns

Common nouns are all the nouns that are not
proper nouns. A common noun may name anybody
or anything that is not a particular person or thing.

EXAMPLES   COMMON NOUNS   PROPER NOUNS
            man   Jim Two Eagles
            dog   Lassie
            mountain   Mt. Rushmore
            planet   Mars

Singular and Plural Nouns

1b A noun may be singular or plural.

A noun may name one thing. It is called a *sin-*
gular noun if it does.

EXAMPLES   human, animal, vegetable, orange,
                      tree, man, woman

A noun may name more than one thing. It is called a *plural noun.*

EXAMPLES   humans, animals, vegetables,
                      oranges, trees, men, women

Most singular nouns add the letter **s** to form their plurals.

EXAMPLES   cat/cat**s**, dog/dog**s**, idea/idea**s**

EXERCISE 4   The following nouns are all singular. Number a sheet of paper from 1 to 10 and write down the nouns. Then rewrite each noun to make it plural.

EXAMPLE   dog

                      dogs

1. shadow   6. hit
2. ear   7. shirt
3. apple   8. blouse
4. idea   9. trick
5. sauce   10. ball

Singular nouns that end in the letters **s, x, ch,** and **sh** may be made into plural nouns by adding the letters **es.**

EXAMPLES   bus/bus**es**, gas/gas**es**, ax/ax**es**,
                      box/box**es**, march/march**es**,
                      pitch/pitch**es**, bush/bush**es**

EXERCISE 5 Some of the following nouns are singular. Some are plural. Number a sheet of paper from 1 to 10. Rewrite each noun. Make the singular nouns plural and the plural nouns singular.

EXAMPLE persons

person

1. dish
2. fox
3. tanks
4. sashes
5. clock

6. barns
7. churches
8. glass
9. wax
10. batches

Possessive Nouns

1c   **A noun can show that something else belongs to it or is related to it.**

When a noun shows that something else belongs to it, it shows possession. This form of the noun is called the *possessive case.*

EXAMPLES   Jean's hat (the hat belongs to Jean)
Tom's glove (the glove belongs to Tom)
the owl's hoot (the hoot of the owl)
the dawn's early light (the early light of dawn)

Form the possessive case of most singular nouns by adding an apostrophe (') and the letter **s**.

EXAMPLES   Dave's treat   lion's growl
Janet's move   girl's bike

Form the possessive case of a plural noun that ends in the letter **s** by adding only an apostrophe.

EXAMPLES girls' laughter   boys' club
          workers' employer   lions' den

EXERCISE 6 Each of the following sentences is written without the correct possessive case. Rewrite each sentence and supply the correct possessive marks.

EXAMPLE   A ducks foot is like a soft paddle.

A duck's foot is like a soft paddle.

1. Most birds wings are built for flying.
2. Some of the worlds best swimmers are birds.
3. In some ways, a penguins body is better suited to the water than to the air.
4. A penguins ability to swim has now replaced its ability to fly.
5. Another of natures swimming birds is the puffin.
6. A puffins wings are clumsy things.
7. Puffins, however, are among the worlds best catchers of fish.
8. With a swimmers skill, they often catch as many as a dozen fish in one dive.

EXERCISE 7 Following are ten singular and plural nouns. Number a sheet of paper from 1 to 10. Use the possessive form of each noun in a sentence of your own.

EXAMPLE   Brown

The Brown's dog howls every night.

1. Smith   6. mothers
2. buses   7. Susan
3. Alex   8. lizard
4. cougars   9. Jinx
5. school   10. Cindy

Compound Nouns

Certain nouns, called *compound nouns,* are made up of two or more words used together to name a single person or thing. Some compound nouns are written as single words, some are written as two or more words, and some are written with a hyphen mark (-) between words.

> EXAMPLES   pancake, football, folk song, goal
>   post, balance of power,
>   mother-in-law, tune-up

Compound nouns form their possessive and plural forms in special ways.

Ways of writing compound nouns are changing. The best way to be certain how to write a compound word is to look it up in a dictionary.

PRONOUNS

1d   A pronoun is a word used to take the place of a noun or a noun word group.

Look at these sentences.

> EXAMPLES   *Luis* waved to *Maria.*
>   *He* waved to *her*.

The old tractor slid into the ditch.
It slid into the ditch.

In the first pair of sentences above, the pronouns *he* and *her* stand for the proper nouns *Luis* and *Maria*. In the second pair, the pronoun *it* stands for the entire word group, *the old tractor*.

Here is a list of common pronouns next to some of the nouns they can stand for:

NOUNS	PRONOUNS
car, bus	it
dimes, horses	they
Nancy Wright, girl	she
Benny Trotter, boy	he
(the person speaking)	I
(the person spoken to)	you

EXERCISE 8   Number a sheet of paper from 1 to 6. Each of the following sentences has a pronoun in it. Next to each number write the pronoun from the sentence.

EXAMPLE   Tractors are not fast, but they can pull a heavy load.

they

1. Transportation moves people where they want to go.
2. Rapid transit moves people fast, but it is expensive to operate.
3. The cost is also high to get it started.
4. If a man works in the city but lives outside, he needs rapid transit.

5. If a woman works downtown in a large city but lives uptown, she needs rapid transit.
6. Only when you live and work in one place is rapid transportation of little use.

EXERCISE 9 Rewrite each of the following sentences. Replace the underlined single noun or the noun word group with a pronoun.

EXAMPLE The two cows stood in the rain.

They stood in the rain.

1. What happens to a city newspaper as the newspaper goes through a day?
2. Suppose old newspapers could talk about what happens as the newspapers are thrown out.
3. Imagine Terry Times is an old newspaper that can talk so that Terry Times can tell his story.
4. I was a new newspaper Friday morning when a young woman bought me as the young woman was going to work.
5. Because so many other people crowded on the bus, the other people made it hard for her to read me.
6. The woman and I were pushed and bumped in the bus.
7. When the woman got to her office, the woman put me on a table in the lunch room.
8. People came in and out all day, but the people never looked at me.
9. A man sat down near me, yet the man ate only a quick lunch.
10. Late that night two cleaning people did what the cleaning people had to do, I guess—they threw me out!

Personal Pronouns

1e   A personal pronoun stands for a noun or noun word group that names a particular person, place, or thing.

The pronouns you used in Exercises 8 and 9 are all personal pronouns. Personal pronouns have several forms. Here is a list of them:

	SINGULAR	PLURAL
First Person (the one talking)	I	We
Second Person (the one being talked to)	you	you
Third Person (the one being talked about)	he, she, it	they

EXERCISE 10   On a separate piece of paper write six sentences. In each sentence use at least one of the eight personal pronouns listed above. Underline each personal pronoun.

1f   A personal pronoun can show that something belongs to someone or to something.

See Case,
p. 254   The *possessive case* of a personal pronoun is formed in the following ways:

POSSESSIVE PRONOUNS

Singular	Plural
my, mine	our, ours
your, yours	your, yours
his	
her, hers	their, theirs
it, its	

EXAMPLES Skip is *my* trained frog. Skip is *mine*.

Is that *your* frog? Is that frog *yours*?

Someone ate *her* frog. Someone ate *hers*.

We won't eat *our* frog. We won't eat *ours*.

She wants to buy *your* frog. She wants to buy *yours*.

They traded *their* frog for a cat. They traded *theirs* for a cat.

EXERCISE 11 Write the following sentences, using the possessive forms of the pronouns in parentheses to fill in the blanks.

EXAMPLE That giant polywog is _____ . (we)

That giant polywog is ours.

1. A bat is a strange creature who likes to spend _____ active time at night. (it)
2. _____ only knowledge of bats is what I read in books. (I)
3. A bat rests in the daytime and seeks _____ food at night. (it)

4. _____ bodies are mouselike. (they)
5. Their hearing is much better than _____ . (we)
6. But our vision is better than _____ . (they)
7. A vampire bat uses _____ sharp teeth to puncture skin. (it)
8. _____ bite is usually painless. (it)
9. For most of us, bats are one of _____ world's most frightening animals. (we)
10. To most bats, humans are probably _____ most frightening enemy. (they)

EXERCISE 12 Copy the sentences below. Fill in the blanks with correct personal pronoun forms. Several different answers are possible for some of the sentences.

EXAMPLES   Jim left _____ dog at home, but Beth brought _____ .

Jim left our dog at home, but Beth brought hers.

or

Jim left his dog at home, but Beth brought hers.

_____ all went to our houses.

We all went to our houses.

1. _____ were going to Marine World Park.
2. _____ is the only sea life aquarium near _____ homes.

3. _____ had to take a train to get there.
4. _____ all took _____ lunches with us.
5. _____ little brother ate _____ lunch on
   _____ train trip there.
6. Then _____ thought _____ would have to
   share _____ lunch with _____ .
7. As it turned out, _____ all shared _____
   lunches with _____ .
8. Sometimes _____ wish _____ would join the
   trained seals.
9. Of course, _____ don't really wish that would
   happen to _____ .
10. But you know how annoying little brothers can
    be sometimes, don't _____ ?

ADJECTIVES

1g **An adjective is a word used to modify or
describe a noun or pronoun.**

Use an adjective to tell *what kind* of a person,
place, or thing you mean. Use an adjective to tell
which one, how much, or *how many.*

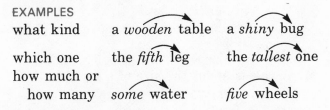

EXAMPLES
what kind   a *wooden* table   a *shiny* bug

which one   the *fifth* leg   the *tallest* one
how much or
   how many   *some* water   *five* wheels

Adjectives may occur several different places
in a sentence. An adjective may appear directly before a noun.

EXAMPLE An *old* tree fell down.

Sometimes two adjectives come together in front of the noun.

EXAMPLE   The *rusty, squeaky* gate scared me.

Adjectives can also come later in a sentence.

EXAMPLE   The glass is *tall*.

See Sentences, pp. 79–80

In this position the adjective is called an *adjective completer* because it completes the meaning of the noun or pronoun to which it refers.

Three short adjectives are used very often. They are the words *a, an,* and *the*. These three adjectives are called *articles*. You will probably find at least one article in every sentence you read, write, or speak.

EXERCISE 13. Copy the following sentences. Underline the adjectives, then circle the nouns or pronouns that they modify. Draw an arrow from each adjective to the noun it describes. Do not underline the articles *a, an,* and *the*. Skip a line between each sentence.

EXAMPLE   The yak is a strange animal.

The yak is a strange animal.

1. A yak is about the size of a small bull.
2. It is hairy.
3. It even has a hairy tail.
4. People in Tibet train the yaks to do hard work.
5. The milk of the yak makes good butter.
6. Tibetans keep the butter in skin bags.
7. They kill fat yaks for meat.

8. Sometimes people eat raw meat after they have dried it.
9. The long, black hair of the yak is woven into strong ropes.
10. The sturdy yak has been a great help to hard-working people living in the high mountains.

EXERCISE 14 Copy the following sentences. Underline the adjectives and circle the nouns or pronouns that they modify. Draw an arrow from each adjective to the noun or pronoun it describes. Do not underline the articles *a, an,* and *the.* Skip a line between each sentence.

EXAMPLE Look at the large bird in the tall tree.

Look at the large bird in the tall tree.

1. I saw a funny cartoon yesterday.
2. It showed a large bird with green wings sitting in a tall tree.
3. Along came a young cat wearing a wrinkled coat.
4. The sly cat said, "Hello, big bird."
5. The bird answered in a deep voice, "You look like a bad cat."
6. "I am hungry," came the quick answer.
7. The strange bird flapped its large wings.
8. "I had three cats for breakfast," the huge bird said.
9. The cat stood and looked with round eyes and pointed ears.
10. Then the cat took a quick walk.

Comparison of Adjectives

1h An adjective may change form to show how one thing compares with another.

Fast is an adjective in the *positive* form. It is used to describe one thing, such as a *fast car*. To compare two things, add the letters **er**, for example, the word *faster,* as in *That jet is faster than a car.* This form is called the *comparative.*

> EXAMPLES This is a *warm* spot. (positive form)
>
> That is a *warmer* spot.
> (comparative form)

To show comparison of three or more things, add the letters **est** to most adjectives. This form is called the *superlative.*

> EXAMPLES This is an *old* tree. (positive form)
>
> This is the *oldest* tree in the woods.
> (superlative form)

Sometimes the last letter of an adjective is doubled when the comparative or superlative form is used.

> EXAMPLES big   bigger   biggest
>
> hot   hotter   hottest

EXERCISE 15 Copy the following sentences. Write the correct choice in the blank.

> EXAMPLE Sue's hair is _____ than Carol's.
> (long/longer/longest)
>
> *Sue's hair is longer than Carol's.*

1. Today is _____ than yesterday. (hot/hotter/hottest)
2. The cheetah is one of the _____ land animals of all. (fast/faster/fastest)
3. A yak is _____ than a gopher. (big/bigger/biggest)
4. Lights in the city are _____ than lights in the country. (bright/brighter/brightest)
5. The brontosaurus was the _____ dinosaur of all. (large/larger/largest)
6. The unicorn was a _____ animal in old stories. (rare/rarer/rarest)
7. A rabbit is _____ than a turtle. (quick/quicker/quickest)
8. The blue whale is the _____ creature ever to live on earth. (long/longer/longest)
9. Rock music is _____ than chamber music. (loud/louder/loudest)
10. The redwood tree is the _____ plant known. (old/older/oldest)

Long adjectives, like *beautiful* and *modern*, do not add the letters **er** and **est**. Use *more* and *most* in front of them to show comparisons.

EXAMPLES She is *more* musical than her older sister.
Their mother is the *most* musical woman in town.

EXERCISE 16 Copy the following sentences on a piece of paper. Write the correct form of the adjective in parentheses in the blank by adding *more* or *most* to it.

EXAMPLE He acted _____ than his brother.
(upset)

He acted more upset than his brother.

1. Mae was _____ than her brother of finding the treasure. (hopeful)
2. She found the last clue the _____ of all. (interesting)
3. Joe thought it was the _____ hunt he had ever known. (foolish)
4. He was _____ than Mae. (tired)
5. When she promised to share half the treasure with him, he became _____ to continue hunting. (willing)

EXERCISE 17 Copy the following sentences. Fill in the blanks with the correct form of the adjective. In some sentences, you will have to use the word *more* or *most* before the adjective. Underline the adjectives you have added in the sentences.

EXAMPLE The wet earth produced the _____ flowers I have ever seen. (beautiful)

The wet earth produced the most beautiful flowers I have ever seen.

1. We saw some _____ clouds late yesterday afternoon. (large)
2. Some small clouds were _____ than the large ones. (close)
3. The large clouds looked _____ than the small ones. (dark)

4. The dark clouds grew _____ and came nearer. (big)

5. Soon a _____ rain started to fall. (hard)

6. The air became _____ than it had been. (cold)

7. A sudden bolt of lightning looked _____ than any of us had ever seen. (brilliant)

8. The next two lightning flashes appeared to be the _____ we had seen. (sensational)

9. Heavy rain was followed by even _____ hail. (heavy)

10. It was the _____ storm anyone could imagine. (spectacular)

REVIEW EXERCISE A Nouns, Pronouns, and Adjectives

The following story has blank spaces where nouns, pronouns, and adjectives belong. Each blank space has a letter that stands for the missing part of speech: N for noun, P for pronoun, and A for adjective.

Write the complete story on another sheet of paper. You may use words from the lists following the story to fill in the blanks.

ALI BABA AND THE FORTY THIEVES

Ali Baba had no money. _P_ was a _A_ man. One day _P_ went to the forest to cut _N_ . He planned to sell the _N_ to get _N_ .

Suddenly he saw forty _A_ men coming toward _P_ . He knew they were robbers. He quickly hid from _P_ . They stopped in front of a cave. __P__ was blocked by a __A__ rock. One __A__ man said, "Open sesame!" The __A__ rock rolled away. The men went in, but soon __P__ came out. The leader said, "Close sesame," and the __N__ closed up the __N__ . Then the __N__ left.

Ali went up to the __A__ cave. __P__ said, "Open sesame!" The huge __N__ rolled away. Then Ali entered the cave. Inside he saw __N__ filled with __A__ __N__ and __A__ __N__ .

NOUNS	PRONOUNS	ADJECTIVES
wood	he	poor
money	it	fierce
rock	they	ugly
boulder	him	large
cave	them	giant
hole		huge
men		secret
robbers		hidden
bags		old
jars		shiny
coins		gold
jewels		
pieces		

REVIEW EXERCISE B Singular and Plural Possessives

Write out the following lists of nouns in four columns on a separate piece of paper. Supply the missing forms in each column. The first one is done for you.

NOUNS

Singular Form	Plural Form	Singular Possessive	Plural Possessive
1. apple	*apples*	*apple's*	*apples'*
2. lamp	_____	_____	_____
3. country	_____	_____	_____
4. monkey	_____	_____	_____
5. woman	_____	_____	_____
6. child	_____	_____	_____

REVIEW EXERCISE C Pronouns

Write the following sentences on a separate sheet of paper. Replace each underlined word or group of words with a pronoun.

EXAMPLE **A fingernail is softer when <u>the fingernail</u> is wet.**

A fingernail is softer when it is wet.

1. Water is necessary for humans because <u>water</u> makes up a large part of the body.
2. The body's organs work only when the <u>body's organs</u> are supplied with food, water, and oxygen.
3. Water alone is not enough because <u>water</u> supplies no energy.
4. Energy is provided by food and oxygen when <u>food and oxygen</u> combine.
5. Julie told me about this when <u>Julie</u> was in science class.
6. David said the same things when <u>David</u> was in the class.

REVIEW EXERCISES D   Adjectives

Each of the following sentences has two or more adjectives in it. Number a sheet of paper from 1 to 10. Next to each number, write the adjectives that appear in that sentence. Do not write the articles *a, an,* or *the.*

EXAMPLE   A hot, dry wind was blowing on the plains.

1. The long day came to an end with a red sunset.
2. The fiery sun had heated the brown earth.
3. A strong wind had blown the loose dust into a huge cloud.
4. The dusty cloud gave a brown color to the blue sky.
5. The bright sun was turned into a dull, red ball.
6. Dry plants dropped to touch the hard earth.
7. Lost cattle wandered in small circles.
8. They could find no green grass nor fresh water.
9. Old farmers could not remember such a bad year.
10. The terrible drought brought serious problems to the unhappy people.

REVIEW EXERCISE E   Using Adjectives to Compare

Copy the following sentences on a sheet of paper. Fill in each blank with the correct form of the adjective in parentheses. You may have to use *more* or *most* with some adjectives. Underline the adjectives you add to the sentences. Draw an arrow from each adjective to the noun or pronoun it modifies.

> EXAMPLE One of the _____ resources to
> conserve is water. (important)
>
> *One of the most important resources to conserve is water.*

1. Fresh water is _____ than salt water. (valuable)
2. Some water is _____ than other water. (fresh)
3. Rivers that flow into the ocean become _____ as they reach the sea. (salty)
4. Some parts of the world have a _____ need for fresh water than others do. (great)
5. Oddly, the _____ need is where there is plenty of water. (great)
6. This is in the middle of the ocean on a ship taking a _____ voyage. (long)
7. People on board might as well be in the middle of the _____ desert in the world. (dry)
8. The ocean has no _____ water than the desert. (fresh)

CHAPTER

2

PARTS OF SPEECH

**Verbs, Adverbs, Prepositions, Conjunctions,
Interjections**

In Chapter 1 you saw how three of the eight parts of speech work. This chapter presents the other five parts of speech.

Some of the most interesting words you may use to give or ask information tell about actions, such as *leaped, plunged, bellowed, moaned,* or *scrunched.* Action words belong to the part of speech called a *verb.* Every sentence you speak or write must contain at least one verb.

Other parts of speech are necessary in sentences as well. *Adverbs* modify the action of verbs. *Prepositions* show special relationships among words. *Conjunctions* tie words or groups of words together. *Interjections* express feeling. All of these parts of speech are explained in this chapter. Study them to find ways to improve your use of the English language.

VERBS

2a **A verb is a word used to tell what happens or exists.**

EXAMPLES 1. Champions *win* more than they
          lose.
          2. Harry *held* the cup high.
          3. Arnold *is* happy.
          4. Effie *seems* happy, too.

The two main types of verbs are *action verbs* and *linking verbs*. Action verbs are used in the first two sentences above. Linking verbs are used in sentences 3 and 4.

Action Verbs

(1) **An action verb tells what someone or something does.**

EXAMPLES Inez *runs* every day
          [*Runs* tells what Inez does.]

          Jim *swam.*
          [*Swam* tells what Jim did.]

          Helen *ate* lunch.
          [*Ate* tells what Helen did.]

          Abe *stumbled.*
          [*Stumbled* tells what Abe did.]

EXERCISE 1 Number a sheet of paper from 1 to 12. Next to each number write the action verb in each sentence.

EXAMPLE   Jennifer enters her horse Koko in
           barrel races.

enters

1. Koko runs fast.
2. He spins on his haunches.
3. Jennifer holds tight.
4. She flicks the reins.
5. Koko plunges to the right.
6. He cuts the corner sharply.
7. Now he rears in excitement.
8. Jennifer pulls the reins.
9. She digs her heels into Koko.
10. He races for the finish.
11. The judge calls the time.
12. Jennifer hugs Koko.

Linking Verbs

**(2) A linking verb expresses a state of being or
links someone or something to words that
complete its meaning.**

A linking verb often begins a description about
someone or something. The verb links or ties a person, place, or thing to other words that complete the
description.

Some common linking verbs are *am, is, are,
become, seem,* and *look.*

EXAMPLES   The earth *is* round.
           [The linking verb *is* begins a
           description of the earth.]

Giraffes *are* tall animals.
[*Are* links *giraffes* to the word *animals* that tells what giraffes are.]

A clown *looks* funny.
[*Looks* is the linking verb. It helps tell what a clown is like. It links *clown* to *funny*.]

EXERCISE 2 Number a sheet of paper from 1 to 10. Next to each number write the linking verb in the sentence.

EXAMPLE Ice is cold.

is

1. Fire is hot.
2. The forest fire was dangerous.
3. The flames seemed huge.
4. The smoke grew thick.
5. Trees became giant torches.
6. Firefighters were tired.
7. The situation appeared bad.
8. It was a difficult problem.
9. A heavy rainstorm seemed the only answer.
10. Rain was the fire extinguisher.

Hint: Remember that a linking verb joins with another word or words to describe a person, place, or thing. An action verb helps tell of something that happens or has happened.

EXERCISE 3　Number a sheet of paper from 1 to 10. List the verbs in each sentence. After each verb identify it as either *action* or *linking*.

EXAMPLES　That girl is very angry.

is, linking

A wolf in a corner fights savagely.

fights, action

1. Baseball is an athletic contest.
2. Many people watch the games.
3. To them, baseball seems exciting.
4. Others avoid baseball.
5. To them, the games are dull.
6. Nine players play on a team.
7. A pitcher throws the baseball to a catcher.
8. Four infielders and three outfielders complete the team.
9. At least one other person helps in baseball.
10. That person, the umpire, is not always popular.

EXERCISE 4　Write five sentences with action verbs. Here are some verbs you can use.

trot	drive	climb
hit	walk	fly
move	put	fall

EXERCISE 5　Write five sentences with linking verbs. Here are some verbs you can use.

am	sound	taste
are	seem	become
appear	was	smell

The verbs you have been studying are *main verbs*. They do the main work of telling what someone did or what something is like. Sometimes main verbs have *helping verbs*. The main verb and its helping verb or verbs are called the *complete verb*, or *verb phrase*.

See Phrases, pp. 62–63

Helping Verbs

(3) **A helping verb helps the main verb tell what happens or what exists.**

MAIN VERB WITHOUT HELPING VERB	MAIN VERB WITH HELPING VERB
run	*has* run, *had* run
tumble	*did* tumble, *will* tumble
jump	*does* jump, *could* jump

These are some of the helping verbs you may use with main verbs:

(I)	*am, was, can, have, had, may*
(you)	*are, were, could, might, will*
(it)	*is, has, would, should, does*

EXERCISE 6 Number a sheet of paper from 1 to 8. Next to each number write the helping verb and the main verb in the sentence. Draw a line under each helping verb.

EXAMPLE   Inez will swim across the pool.

will swim

1. Inez and Marie will take a lesson on Saturday.
2. Inez can float on her stomach.
3. Marie has had a lesson already.
4. She does float on her stomach and on her back.
5. She might kick her way across the pool.
6. Inez should practice her kick more.
7. Then she could get across the pool, too.
8. Both girls would enjoy the water more after several lessons.

Tense

2b Most verbs change form to show a change in time.

Most verbs have two forms to show a change in time. One form shows *present time*. The other form shows *past time*. The time shown by a verb is called its *tense*.

EXAMPLES   Now I *remember* her. (present tense)
Then I *remembered* her. (past tense) *

A verb also can show time in the future. This is called its *future tense*. A common way of showing future tense is by using the helping verbs *shall* or *will* with the present tense form of the main verb.

EXAMPLES I *shall see* Claudia.

We *will trim* the hedge.

To show past tense, verbs are called either *regular* or *irregular*.

Regular Verbs

(1) Regular verbs add *d* or *ed* to the infinitive to form their past tense.

The *infinitive* is the base form of a verb. It takes the word *to* in front of it.

EXAMPLES to *run*   to *hold*

to *go*   to *stay*

EXAMPLES	INFINITIVE	PAST TENSE
	aid	aided
	believe	believed
	borrow	borrowed
	move	moved
	stop	stopped
	watch	watched

Irregular Verbs

(2) Irregular verbs may change form to show past tense, but they do not add *ed* or *d*.

EXAMPLES	INFINITIVE	PAST TENSE
	begin	began
	eat	ate
	fly	flew

go	went
run	ran
hit	hit
swim	swam

EXERCISE 7 Number a sheet of paper from 1 to 20. Write the past forms of each of the following verbs. Then put an *R* or an *I* next to each verb to show whether it is *regular* or *irregular*. If you are not sure about a verb, look it up in a dictionary.

EXAMPLES **fix**

fixed, R

choose

chose, I

1. break	6. attempt	11. try	16. flirt
2. quit	7. time	12. ask	17. get
3. sing	8. tease	13. feel	18. fill
4. walk	9. plan	14. fish	19. shoot
5. spell	10. beg	15. grow	20. hold

ADVERBS

2c An adverb usually modifies a verb.

An adverb can tell *when* something happened.

EXAMPLES *Yesterday* Wylda Burbank gave a party.
[When did she give the party? Answer: *yesterday*.]

Elmer Bean arrived *early*.
[When did he arrive? Answer:
early.]

Archie Bacon arrived *late*.
[When did he arrive? Answer: *late*.]

The words *ever, not,* and *never* are also adverbs. *Not* and *never* give an opposite meaning to the verb.

EXAMPLES   I can go this evening.

I ca*nnot* go this evening.

He will come soon.

He will *never* come.

EXERCISE 8 Copy the following sentences. In each sentence underline the adverb that tells *when*. Some sentences have more than one adverb. Draw an arrow from the adverb to the main verb that it modifies.

EXAMPLE   Terry Dumday brushes her teeth
daily.

Terry Dumday brushes her teeth daily.

1. Mr. Fitzwhistle walks his kangaroo occasionally.
2. Worried neighbors stopped him yesterday.
3. They demanded that he cease the practice immediately.
4. Today, Mr. Fitzwhistle is walking his tiger, and the neighbors leave him alone now.
5. "Tomorrow," he says, "I will take my crocodile down to the pool."

An adverb can tell *where* something happened.

EXAMPLES   She slept *upstairs*.
[Where did she sleep? Answer: *upstairs*.]

Please sleep *here*.
[Where will the sleeping take place? Answer: *here*.]

EXERCISE 9   Copy the following sentences. In each sentence underline the adverb or adverbs that tell *where*. Draw an arrow from the adverb to the main verb it modifies. Skip a line between each sentence.

EXAMPLE   The skunk lives there.

The skunk lives there.

1. I am a master of disguise, and I wander everywhere.
2. They have looked for me high and low.
3. They have found me nowhere.
4. People search for me outside.
5. I hide inside.
6. They ask for me here.
7. I appear elsewhere in a walrus disguise.
8. I walk downtown, dressed as a parking meter.

An adverb can tell *how* someone did something, *how* something happened, *how much* of the action was involved, or *how often* the action occurred.

EXAMPLES   LaDoris Belcher waited *quietly*.

[How did LaDoris wait? Answer: *quietly*.]

She spoke *firmly*.
[How did she speak? Answer: *firmly*.]

EXERCISE 10 Copy the following sentences. In each sentence underline every adverb that tells *how, how long,* or *how often* something happened. Draw an arrow from each adverb to the verb it modifies.

EXAMPLE   The waters rose steadily.

The waters rose steadily.

1. Max Maxwell dreamed he drifted quietly on a calm lake.
2. A large sea serpent appeared mysteriously.
3. Max rowed furiously.
4. The serpent swam calmly and asked, "Max, why leave hurriedly?"
5. Max smiled nervously and dropped his oars quickly.
6. "You swim well," Max said softly as he politely offered the serpent a small tuna sandwich.
7. The serpent swam endlessly in circles around the boat.
8. It finally disappeared, so Max carefully picked up his oars and rowed swiftly to shore.

EXERCISE 11 Copy the following sentences. In each sentence underline the adverb and draw an arrow to the verb it modifies. Skip a line between each sentence.

EXAMPLE The penguin marched downstairs.

The penguin marched downstairs.

1. Max turned the door handle nervously.
2. He opened the door completely.
3. Max looked inside.
4. Then he entered the room cautiously.
5. "I thought I heard noises here," he said.
6. He looked briefly at everything in the room.
7. He suddenly saw a small penguin.
8. "Care for a yogurt bar?" the bird asked calmly.
9. "Why, yes," Max answered. "I eat them often."
10. "You froze this solidly," said Max as he bit on the yogurt bar.

Hint: An adverb tells *when, where, how, how much,* or *how often* the action occurs.

2d   Adverbs help compare actions of verbs.

Most short adverbs add **er** and **est** to show comparison. When only two actions are compared, use the ending **er**. When three or more actions are compared, use **est**.

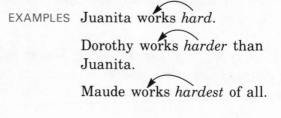

EXAMPLES Juanita works *hard.*

Dorothy works *harder* than Juanita.

Maude works *hardest* of all.

EXERCISE 12 Copy the following five sentences. Underline each adverb, then draw an arrow from each adverb to the verb it modifies.

EXAMPLE Earl Egg jumps higher than H. Dumpty.

*Carl Egg jumps higher
than H. Dumpty.*

1. Cabot Carrot sees farther than most of his friends.
2. Odetta, however, sees farthest of all.
3. Her eyes grow larger when she looks into the distance.
4. They glow bluer than robins' eggs.
5. No one I have met has eyes that shine brighter.

Adverbs ending in *ly* do not change spelling to show comparison. These adverbs take the words *more* or *most* in front of them.

EXAMPLES helpfully, more helpfully, most helpfully
tenderly, more tenderly, most tenderly

EXERCISE 13 Copy each sentence and fill in the blank by writing the correct form of the adverb you see next to each sentence.

EXAMPLE The wind blew _____ this morning than last night. (forcefully)

more forcefully

1. Of all the recorder players I have ever heard, you play the _____ . (beautifully)
2. If you practice _____ than you do now, you could go to a music school. (regularly)
3. You will improve _____ there than if you continue on your own. (rapidly)
4. You will learn to play _____ than you do now. (skillfully)
5. As the old masters say, "Not even the triangle echoes _____ than the song of the recorder." (powerfully)

The adverb *well* changes its form in special ways. Here are its forms.

well	Da-jen sings *well*.
better	Joan sings *better* than Da-jen.
best	Marie sings *best* of all.

EXERCISE 14 Number a sheet of paper from 1 to 6. Write the correct form of *well* to fill the blank.

EXAMPLE   Thistleworth dances _____ than Mr. Fogg.

better

1. Horses trot _____ than parakeets.
2. Parakeets fly _____ than anteaters.
3. Moths also fly _____ .
4. Some Americans eat _____ than others.
5. The French, in general, also eat _____ .
6. Italians, some people say, eat _____ of all.

2e An adverb sometimes modifies an adjective or another adverb.

See Adjective, p. 252

EXAMPLES   He has an unusually long surfboard.
            [The adverb *unusually* modifies the adjective *long*.]

            He swam very quickly.
            [The adverb *very* modifies the adverb *quickly*.]

EXERCISE 15 Number a sheet of paper from 1 to 5. Copy the adverb in each sentence. After each adverb, write the adjective or adverb it modifies.

EXAMPLE   Mae is a much faster runner than Jamie.

much, faster

1. Softball can be a surprisingly fast game.
2. A good pitcher throws an extremely hard pitch.
3. Although the playing field is much smaller than a regular baseball field, a good batter can hit a home run.
4. Both men and women play softball very well.
5. The crowds like to see an especially close game.

PREPOSITIONS

2f A preposition is a word used to relate a following noun or pronoun to some other words in a sentence.

See Noun, p. 266
See Pronoun, p. 270

EXAMPLES Mom took a walk *after* lunch.
[The preposition *after* relates *lunch* to *took a walk*.]

The football is lying *under* the car.
[The preposition *under* relates *car* to *is lying*.]

The stories of Lewis Carroll are known *to* me.
[The preposition *of* relates *Lewis Carroll* to *stories*. The preposition *to* relates *me* to *are known*.]

Prepositions often help to show relationships of time, place, manner, or kind.

EXAMPLES			MANNER
TIME		PLACE	OR KIND
after	about	beside	by
before	above	between	except
since	across	in	like
until	among	off	of
during	around	over	for
	at	through	with
	behind	under	without
	below	up	from
	to	on	
	toward	down	
	against	within	

EXERCISE 16 Number a sheet of paper from 1 to 10. After each number write each preposition you find in the sentence. Some sentences have more than one preposition.

EXAMPLE Millie ran into the apartment.

/ Into /

1. Felicita and José were sitting in the living room.
2. Mac was standing by the kitchen door.
3. Millie jumped over a pillow lying on the floor.
4. She stood still after her jump.
5. Felicita and José glanced toward Mac.
6. They all had funny looks on their faces.
7. The play's director was sitting in a seat near the stage.
8. She walked toward the stage.
9. "Let's take that again," she said as she stepped on the stage.
10. The actors returned to their places.

Object of the Preposition

A preposition in a sentence is always followed by a noun or pronoun. The noun or pronoun is called the *object of the preposition.* In the following examples, the prepositions are italicized. The arrow points to the object of the preposition.

EXAMPLES The bell rang *at* midnight.

It meant we were *on* time.

We slipped away *under* cover

of thick, silent darkness.

EXERCISE 17 Number a sheet of paper from 1 to 5. Following are five sentences containing prepositions and their objects. After each number, write the preposition and its object. Underline each preposition you have written.

> EXAMPLE   The whistle blows at midday.

at midday

1. The assembly line stops at noon.
2. Some workers go home for their meal.
3. Others carry their lunches in tin boxes.
4. They find sandwiches in them.
5. Their sandwiches are packed in plastic.

CONJUNCTIONS

2g   A conjunction is a word used to connect words or groups of words.

The most common conjunctions are *and, but, for, nor,* and *or.*

Conjunctions connect words or word groups.

> EXAMPLES   The dog runs back *and* forth.
> [*and* connects the words *back* and *forth.*]
>
> June ran up the stairs *and* into the house.
> [*and* connects the groups of words *up the stairs* and *into the house.*]
>
> Wanda will go *but* Marie will stay home.
> [*but* connects the word groups *Wanda will go* and *Marie will stay home.*]

EXERCISE 18   Number a sheet of paper from 1 to 5. The conjunctions have been left out of the five following sentences. After each number, write the conjunction that belongs in the blank.

> EXAMPLE   Young plums are bitter _____ hard.
>
> *and*

1. Next Saturday we plan to lock the house _____ drive to town.
2. Harriet wants to eat dinner at Luigi's, _____ Grace hopes to dine at Wong's.
3. We can have a five-course Italian dinner _____ eat a seven-course Chinese meal.
4. We could not eat both, _____ that would be too much.
5. Neither Harriet _____ I know much about Chinese food.

EXERCISE 19   Number a sheet of paper from 1 to 4. Write four sentences, using conjunctions to connect words or word groups.

> EXAMPLE   Use *and* to connect two nouns.
>
> *Eggs and sausages make a hearty breakfast.*

1. Use *and* to connect two verbs in a sentence.
2. Use *or* to connect two prepositions and their objects in a sentence.
3. Use *but* to connect two adjectives in a sentence.
4. Use *and* to connect two adverbs in a sentence.

INTERJECTIONS

2h   An interjection is a word or group of words used to express strong feeling.

EXAMPLES   *Good heavens!* What a mess this is.
Aha! I caught you.
I could only think, *Oh, wow!*
"Boo!" said the ghost to the
frightened children.

An interjection is often followed by an exclamation mark (!). Sometimes an interjection in the middle of a sentence is set off only by commas.

EXAMPLE   This storm, *worse luck*, has ruined
our vacation.
Professor Sly, *blast his hide*, has
eluded us once again.

EXERCISE 20   Number a sheet of paper from 1 to 4. Next to each number write the interjection in each sentence.

EXAMPLE   "Good grief!" she yelled as soon as
she walked in the door.

Good grief!

1. "Shucks," said the girl, "I just want to be a farmhand."
2. "Will we reach shore? Doggone, we'd better," was all the captain could say as a giant wave tipped the boat on end.
3. "Tarnation!" sputtered the mechanic when his engine coughed and died.
4. "Oh, my heavens," was all we heard.

WORDS AS DIFFERENT PARTS OF SPEECH

2i Some words can be used as different parts of speech.

The English language has some words that serve as more than one part of speech.

EXAMPLES

PLANE
Noun: The *plane* landed at the airfield.
Verb: *Plane* the edge of the board smooth.

AIR
Noun: Breathe some fresh *air.*
Adjective: The *air* mattress is leaking.
Verb: *Air* the blankets in the sun.

Learn how words work as parts of speech in sentences. It is the use of a word that tells its part of speech.

REVIEW EXERCISE A Parts of Speech

The following story has blanks where verbs, adverbs, prepositions, conjunctions, and interjections belong. Each blank has a letter that stands for the missing part of speech: *V* for verbs, *A* for adverbs, *P* for prepositions, *C* for conjunctions, and *I* for interjections.

Write the complete story on another sheet of paper. You may use words from the lists following the story, or you may put in your own words to fill in the blanks.

One day a poor fisherman __V__ his fish net __P__ the sea. Then he __A__ pulled it out. He looked for fish __P__ the net, __C__ he found only a copper jar. When he took the top __P__ the jar, a cloud of smoke __V__ out. The smoke __A__ turned into a giant.

"Prepare to die!" __V__ the giant.

"__I__ !" shouted the fisherman. "What have I done wrong?"

"I have been __V__ in this jar for three hundred years," said the giant __A__ . "I swore that I would __V__ the first person I saw, __C__ you are that person."

The fisherman thought __A__ . "Before I die, may I ask a question?"

"Yes, but ask it __A__ ."

"Is it possible you were inside that jar?" asked the fisherman. "It is not large enough to hold one of your feet."

The giant __A__ changed back into smoke and __V__ into the jar. After the smoke was gone, the fisherman __A__ clapped the lid down tight. The giant __V__ to be set free, but the fisherman only threw the closed jar into the deep sea.

VERBS

throw	threw	rush	rushed
bellow	bellowed	trap	trapped
kill	killed	slip	slipped
beg	begged		

ADVERBS

carefully	slowly	angrily	quickly
speedily	silently	suddenly	

PREPOSITIONS

into   in   off   inside

CONJUNCTIONS

but   and

INTERJECTIONS

Heavens   Gee whiz   Zounds

REVIEW EXERCISE B   Verbs

Number a sheet of paper from 1 to 10. Next to each number write the complete verb in the sentence. After the verb write *AV* if it is an action verb. Write *LV* if it is a linking verb.

EXAMPLE   Trees grow best with plenty of water.

grow, AV

1. Tree roots go deep in the soil.
2. The soil holds water.
3. Water is essential for the trees.
4. The leaves of trees take in carbon dioxide.
5. Leaves are like little food manufacturers.
6. They combine water and carbon dioxide.
7. Sunlight helps the combination.
8. The leaves make food for the tree.
9. They give off oxygen and water.
10. Trees are important for our air.

REVIEW EXERCISE C   Adverbs

Number a sheet of paper from 1 to 10. Next to each number write the verb and the adverb in the sentence. Underline the adverb. Draw an arrow from the adverb to the verb or verbs it modifies.

EXAMPLE   The birds acted strangely this afternoon.

acted strangely

1. They flew quickly from tree to tree.
2. Their wings fluttered nervously.
3. They chirped unendingly.
4. I suddenly noticed the darkness.
5. In the afternoon, the sky darkened gradually.
6. The sun disappeared slowly from view.
7. An eclipse of the sun strangely shadowed the countryside.
8. All the birds immediately grew silent.
9. They mistakenly thought it was night.
10. After the eclipse, the many birds happily flew and sang.

REVIEW EXERCISE D   Analyzing Sentences

Each following sentence has at least one verb, one adverb, one preposition, and one conjunction. Number down the left side of a sheet of paper, 1 to 8. Make four columns on your paper. Put these headings at the top of the columns:

VERB   ADVERB   PREPOSITION   CONJUNCTION

In each column, write one example of a part of speech from each sentence. The first sentence has been done for you as an example.

VERB	ADVERB	PREPOSITION	CONJUNCTION
drove	hurriedly	to	and

1. The two robbers drove hurriedly to the country store and parked their car.
2. One person leaped clumsily from the car, but the other sat at the wheel.
3. The driver in the car watched fearfully, but his companion boldly entered the store.
4. The driver raced the engine of the car impatiently, for he thought his companion was too slow.
5. He thought they might be caught, and he stepped harder on the accelerator.
6. His companion finally emerged from the store and jumped into the car.
7. "Did you get it?" asked the driver, and then he pulled away from the store in a hurry.
8. "Yep," said his companion cheerily, "here are your peanuts, and I've got 'my apple here in my pocket."

PHRASES

Noun Phrases, Prepositional Phrases, Verb Phrases

You have studied how a single word may act as a part of speech. A group of words may also be a part of speech. Suppose someone described a fight to you in this way:

The dogs and cats battled in a howling, screeching, mewing, scratching, biting, rolling, clawing, furry mass!

The group of words *in a howling, screeching, mewing, scratching, biting, rolling, clawing, furry mass* describes how the dogs and cats battled. Together these words serve as an adverb modifying the verb. Instead of a single word, this part of speech is made up of eleven words.

Other groups of words may act together as individual parts of speech. Any group of words that acts as a single part of speech is called a *phrase.*

KINDS OF PHRASES

3a **A phrase is a group of related words used as a single part of speech.**

Three kinds of phrases that are widely used are the *noun phrase,* the *prepositional phrase,* and the *verb phrase.*

Noun Phrases

3b **A noun phrase is a group of related words ending with a noun.**

EXAMPLES *A huge beetle* flew in the window.
[The words *a huge* are related to the noun *beetle.* Together they make a noun phrase. The phrase is used as a noun.]
Andy saw *several more beetles* outside.
[The noun phrase *several more beetles* is used as a noun.]

Remember that a noun phrase is made up of a noun and the words closely related to it. A noun phrase serves as a single part of speech—a noun.

EXERCISE 1 Number a sheet of paper from 1 to 5. Each of the following sentences has a noun phrase. Next to each number on your paper write the noun phrase.

EXAMPLE Jeb took the biggest apple.

the biggest apple

1. Open the back door.
2. Let the bright sunshine come in.
3. We have had ten dark days.
4. The giant snowdrifts crowd in on us.
5. Every sunny ray helps.

Prepositional Phrases

See Preposi-
tion, p. 270;
Noun, p. 266;
Pronoun,
p. 270
3c A prepositional phrase begins with a preposition and usually ends with a noun or pronoun.

The noun or pronoun is called the *object of the preposition*. Words that modify or describe the object are part of the prepositional phrase, but they are not part of the object.

EXAMPLE   She put the jack *into the open trunk*.
[The words *into the open trunk*
make up a prepositional phrase.
Into is a preposition. Its object is
trunk. The words that modify *trunk*
are *the open*.]

Here are more examples of prepositional phrases. Arrows are drawn from the preposition to its object. Note that a preposition may have more than one object.

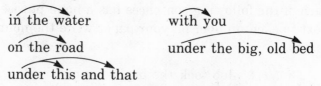

A prepositional phrase is made up of the preposition, its object, and all the modifiers of its object.

Hint: Do not confuse a prepositional phrase beginning with the word *to* with the infinitive form of a verb, for example, *to go*. Remember that a prepositional phrase always has an object.

EXERCISE 2 Number a sheet of paper from 1 to 5. Each of the five following sentences has one or more prepositional phrases. Write each phrase after the number of the sentence in which it appears.

    EXAMPLE   We saw them in the restaurant.

       in the restaurant.

1. They were sitting on a bench.
2. Their coats were under the bench.
3. When they saw us enter, they looked at each other.
4. They quickly grabbed their coats and went out the door.
5. The losers did not want to be near us.

(1) A prepositional phrase may be used as an adjective.

See Adjective, p. 252

    A prepositional phrase used as an adjective modifies a noun or pronoun. The noun or pronoun usually comes just before the prepositional phrase. It is not the object of the preposition.

    When a prepositional phrase is used as an adjective, it helps to answer the question *what kind? which one?* or *how many?*

EXAMPLES   Stories *about haunted houses* scare me.
[The prepositional phrase *about haunted houses* tells what kind of stories scare me.]

The house *by the river* is empty.
[The prepositional phrase *by the river* tells which house is empty.]

EXERCISE 3 Number a sheet of paper from 1 to 15. The following sentences contain prepositional phrases used as adjectives. Next to each number write the prepositional phrase and underline it. Then list the word it modifies.

EXAMPLE No one knew the last people in the house.

in the house, people

1. Is it the house with broken windows?
2. Yes, its windows are gone, and it has a door without hinges.
3. We have heard strange stories about the house.
4. One person in town said she knew the house was haunted.
5. Her brother told her a story of horror.
6. The beginning of the story took place one dark night.
7. He had been fishing all afternoon and had caught several fish of a good size.
8. He thought he would find a quiet resting place near the house.
9. He saw a grassy spot on some high ground.
10. He then ate a little food from his knapsack.

11. He planned to take a nap for half an hour.
12. When he awoke, it was the dark of night.
13. He heard a sound like a low moan.
14. He ran, forgetting his knapsack, his fishing rod, and his string of fish.
15. His fear for his personal safety caused him to leave them.

(2) A prepositional phrase may be used as an adverb. See Adverb, p. 252

    A prepositional phrase used as an adverb modifies a verb, an adjective, or another adverb. When a prepositional phrase is used as an adverb, it helps to answer one of these questions: *When? Where? How? How long? How much?* or *How many?*

EXAMPLES   The owl arrived *after midnight.*
[The prepositional phrase *after midnight* tells *when* the owl arrived.]

It had been housed *in the chimney.*
[The prepositional phrase *in the chimney* tells *where* it had been housed.]

It was captured *by a long noose.*
[The phrase *by a long noose* tells *how* it was captured.]

The owl kept everyone awake *for four hours.*
[The phrase *for four hours* tells *how long* people were kept awake.]

EXERCISE 4 Number a sheet of paper from 1 to 15. Each of the following sentences contains a prepositional phrase used as an adverb. After each number, write the prepositional phrase that appears in the sentence.

EXAMPLE   The ancient Maya civilization has been thoroughly studied by scientists.

by scientists.

1. The Maya Indians lived long ago in Central America.
2. They built their cities in the thick jungle.
3. Most cities were built before the fifth century A.D.
4. By A.D. 800 the Maya had developed a flourishing civilization.
5. Their cities were used for trade and government.
6. But the Maya did not live in the cities.
7. Their jungle homes were placed around the cities.
8. The Maya believed their ancestors came from the sun and the moon.
9. They worshipped sun, moon, and rain gods in many ways.
10. For many years Maya priests studied astronomy and arithmetic.
11. Their records show they could predict an eclipse with accuracy.
12. They made up a writing code used for centuries.
13. This was the only writing code European explorers found in all America.
14. By A.D. 900 the Maya had deserted their cities.
15. In later years their civilization disappeared.

EXERCISE 5 Number a sheet of paper from 1 to 12. Each of the following sentences contains at least one prepositional phrase used as an adjective or an adverb. After each number, write the prepositional phrase or phrases. Then write *adj.* if the phrase is used as an adjective and write *adv.* if it is used as an adverb.

EXAMPLES   Americans eat more than fifteen billion kilograms of meat each year.

of meat, adj.

Farmers raise beef cattle in the country.

in the country, adv.

1. People had always hoped to shorten the sailing route between the Atlantic and the Pacific Oceans.
2. A narrow isthmus in Central America seemed the best place to build a canal.
3. The Panama Canal was completed in 1914.
4. It was the result of much effort.
5. More than 153 million cubic meters of dirt were moved.
6. At one time, 43,000 workers toiled.
7. The bite of a disease-carrying mosquito was an ever-present danger.
8. Sickness and heat caused great trouble for the workers.
9. Medical aid to workers was improved so that they did not suffer greatly.
10. The United States spent 400 million dollars to make the canal a safe passage for ships.

11. Now ships need not sail around South America.
12. Each year as many as 13,000 ships pass through the Panama Canal.

EXERCISE 6   Number a sheet of paper from 1 to 5. Write your own sentences using the following prepositional phrases. Underline each phrase. Draw an arrow to the word it modifies.

EXAMPLE   in the box

Put the candies in the box.

1. by the clock
2. toward the hut
3. of the hill
4. with the curly hair
5. down the well

6. without anger
7. during recess
8. after the rabbit
9. under the ashes
10. within the speed limits

See Verb, p. 273

Verb Phrases

3d   A verb phrase is made up of the main verb and its helpers.

The main verb in a sentence tells of the action or condition of someone or something.

EXAMPLE   Janette *ran* a fast race.

Often the main verb has a helping verb.

EXAMPLE   Janette *had run* a fast race before.

The main verb and its helpers are called a *verb phrase*. The verb phrase may also be called the *complete verb*.

EXERCISE 7 Number a sheet of paper from 1 to 7. Find the verb phrases in the following sentences. Next to each number write the verb phrase from the sentence.

EXAMPLE Willard had left two hours before José.

had left

1. Pistols were first used in the sixteenth century.
2. By the middle of that century the flintlock pistol had been invented.
3. The firing was caused by a piece of flint striking sparks against metal.
4. In the middle of the nineteenth century a good automatic revolver was developed.
5. Samuel Colt, an American, had worked many years to invent his revolver.
6. It was given his name.
7. Today, hundreds of kinds of pistols are known.

REVIEW EXERCISE A   Noun Phrases

Each of the following sentences has one or more noun phrases in it. Number a sheet of paper from 1 to 10. Next to each number write every noun phrase in the sentence.

EXAMPLE The jelly sandwich was smashed.

The jelly sandwich

1. On it Angelica found a large, heavy jar.
2. The paper bag had been lying upside down.

3. The fat jar had pressed the soft sandwich.
4. A jelly smear coated the sandwich bag.
5. The white paper was a different color.
6. Purple grape jelly had left a colorful mess.
7. A white cupcake also had been smeared.
8. Angelica lifted out the crumbly, jellied cake.
9. She planned to throw away the ruined food.
10. But hunger overcame her first plan.

REVIEW EXERCISE B   Prepositional Phrases

Each of the following sentences has at least one prepositional phrase used as an adjective or an adverb. Number a sheet of paper from 1 to 10. Next to each number write the prepositional phrase from the sentence. Draw a line under the preposition. List the word or words to which the phrase refers. Then write *adj.* if the phrase is used as an adjective. Write *adv.* if the phrase is used as an adverb.

EXAMPLE   The archer pulled an arrow from his quiver.

from his quiver, pulled, adv.

1. The king made an announcement to his kingdom.
2. A fair would be held in the town.
3. An archery contest for all comers would be held.
4. Many archers appeared with their bows and arrows.
5. Workmen set up straw targets in a field.

6. The archers lined up at the other end.
7. Each shot an arrow into a target.
8. The final event of the archery competition began between a king's archer and a masked archer.
9. The archer in the mask beat the king's archer.
10. The winner of the competition removed the mask—and revealed a young woman!

REVIEW EXERCISE C Verb Phrases

Number a sheet of paper from 1 to 10. Write the verb phrase from each sentence next to each number.

EXAMPLE The soldiers had attacked the fort.

had attacked

1. Their efforts so far had been unsuccessful.
2. They had rushed the main gates.
3. They were beaten at the gates.
4. They next had crept around the walls.
5. Everywhere they were met with bullets.
6. The defenders had fought better than the attackers.
7. The attackers were forced back again and again.
8. The defenders could rest a little now.
9. A new threat had come, however, in the person of a giant.
10. The giant had begun to put all the soldiers in the play box with the other tin and plastic toys.

REVIEW EXERCISE D　Phrases

Here are ten phrases. Use each phrase in a sentence of your own.

EXAMPLE　in the vault

The banker put the money in the vault.

1. after five o'clock
2. during the night
3. under the street
4. with special tools
5. a tiny speck

6. was placed
7. of the alarm
8. in the darkness
9. were captured
10. the flapping flag

SENTENCES

The Sentence, Sentence Problems

Individual words or groups of words that act as parts of speech can be put together in a useful pattern called a *sentence*. A sentence needs no other words to make it a complete thought.

Sentences must make sense to your listener or reader. If they do not make sense, you may have left out some important part. Or you may have used a wrong part. Make all your sentences make sense to your listeners and readers.

THE SENTENCE

4a A sentence is a group of related words that makes a complete statement.

A sentence is a complete thought. It begins with a capital letter and ends with a period, a question mark, or an exclamation mark.

EXAMPLES Trees grow.
Did you ring?
Bees sting when they are angry.
Look out for that lizard!
Mammals breathe air.

EXERCISE 1 Number a sheet of paper from 1 to 10. Some of the following word groups are sentences. Others are not. Write *S* next to each number of a sentence. Write *N* next to each number that is not a sentence.

1. Funny jokes
2. Went downhill
3. The light shines
4. Gliders glide
5. A gleaming white car
6. Fell from the stove
7. Under strong pressure
8. Jim tossed the pancake
9. Elaine tried to catch it
10. It landed on the table by the eggs

4b A simple sentence must contain a subject and a predicate.

EXAMPLES SUBJECT   PREDICATE
The sun   rises in the morning.
The earth   rotates.
Life   goes on.

(1) The subject is what the sentence tells about.

The *complete subject* is a noun or a pronoun and words that describe the noun or pronoun.

EXAMPLE   These *women* marched to the town hall.

[The noun *women* and the adjective *these* tell *who* marched to the town hall.]

If the subject is removed, the words no longer make a sentence.

EXAMPLE   Marched to the town hall.

The noun or pronoun that is part of the complete subject is called the *simple subject*.

EXAMPLE   These *women* marched to the town hall.

[The noun *women* is the simple subject of this sentence.]

EXERCISE 2   Number a sheet of paper from 1 to 10. Next to each number write the complete subject. Circle the simple subject.

EXAMPLE   Ten tall men led the parade.

Ten tall (men)

1. The small boy placed his nose on the glass.
2. His eyes were grey and thoughtful.
3. His curly hair stood on end.
4. The babysitter called his name.
5. The older woman appeared in the doorway.
6. The silent boy pretended not to see her.
7. His grey eyes were laughing.
8. His game did not fool the babysitter.

9. This German woman understood little boys well.
10. Four others called her their grandmother.

(2) The predicate tells something about the subject.

The *complete predicate* is always a verb and the related words that tell about the subject.

> EXAMPLE　The people *looked angry*.
> [The verb *looked* and the adverb *angry* tell how the people looked.]

If the predicate is removed, the words no longer make a sentence.

> EXAMPLE　The people.

Every complete predicate must contain a verb. The main verb and any helping verbs that make up the complete verb are called the *simple predicate*.

> EXAMPLES　These women *marched to the town hall*.
> [The verb *marched* is the simple predicate of this sentence. The complete predicate is *marched to the town hall*.]
>
> They *were moving swiftly*.
> [The main verb *moving* and the helping verb *were* are the simple predicate of this sentence. The complete predicate is *were moving swiftly*.]

> Hint: A sentence cannot have a subject without a predicate or a predicate without a subject.

EXERCISE 3 Number a sheet of paper from 1 to 12. Next to each number write the complete predicate. Put a box around the complete verb that is the simple predicate.

> EXAMPLE Everyone in our town has heard the news.
>
> $\boxed{\textit{has heard}}$ *the news*

1. Tom has been accused of stealing a pig.
2. Tom is the son of Mr. and Mrs. Piper.
3. The Pipers have thirteen children.
4. Tom is the oldest of them.
5. He has a tree house in a large oak.
6. The pig was seen in his tree house.
7. That pig never had much sense.
8. Tom makes the strangest friends.
9. He does know the difference between man and beast.
10. I asked him about the pig.
11. He whispered his secret to me.
12. "Pigs are nicer!"

EXERCISE 4 Copy the following sentences. Underline each complete subject once and each complete predicate twice. Circle the simple subject. Put a box around the simple predicate.

EXAMPLE Many strange animals live in
Australia.

*Many strange (animals) live
in Australia.*

1. Kangaroos make their home in Australia.
2. They eat grass and leaves from trees.
3. Some kangaroos grow seven feet tall.
4. A large kangaroo runs at a speed of thirty
   miles per hour.
5. It leaps twenty-five feet.
6. A kangaroo is timid by nature.
7. It runs from its enemies.
8. An angry kangaroo fights sometimes.
9. Some people train kangaroos as pets.
10. A baby kangaroo hides in its mother's pouch.

Compound Subject and Compound Predicate

**(3) A sentence with more than one subject has a
      compound subject.**

See Conjunc-
tion, p. 257   The subjects are usually joined by the conjunctions *and, or, nor,* or *but.*

EXAMPLE *The women* and *one old man*
          marched to the town hall.
          [Both the words *women* and *man* are
          the simple subjects because they are
          what the sentence tells about.
          Together these words and their
          modifiers make up the compound
          subject.]

(4) A sentence with more than one verb has a compound predicate.

The verbs are usually joined by the conjunctions *and, or, nor,* or *but.*

EXAMPLE The women and one old man
marched and *sang on their way to
the hall.*
[The two verbs *marched* and *sang*
both describe what the compound
subject of the sentence did. Together,
these verbs and their modifiers
make up the compound predicate in
this sentence.]

Hint: To find the simple predicate of a
sentence, look for the word or words that
tell of the action or begin a description of
someone or something.
To find the simple subject, ask *who* or
what does the action or ask *who* or *what* is
the sentence about.

EXERCISE 5 Number a sheet of paper from 1 to
10. Some of the following sentences have a compound subject. Others do not. Next to each number
write the word or words that make up each simple
subject in each sentence.

EXAMPLE Roots and leaves give life to trees.

Roots, leaves

1. Leaves or needles are found on most trees in North America.
2. Many trees and bushes lose their leaves in the fall.
3. Leaves turn water and air into food.
4. Light and air are necessary for leaves to work.
5. Most of the water comes from the ground.
6. Water and carbon dioxide mix in the leaf.
7. Sunlight helps to do the work of making food.
8. Food for the tree and unused gas are the results of food-making by the tree.
9. The unused gas is oxygen.
10. Humans and animals use the oxygen released by leaves and needles.

EXERCISE 6   Number a sheet of paper from 1 to 10. Some of the following sentences have a compound predicate, others do not. Next to each number write the verb or verbs that make up each simple predicate.

> EXAMPLE   Helen Keller lived and died in darkness and silence.

lived, died

1. At an early age Helen Keller became sick and lost her sight and hearing.
2. She learned little language as a very young girl.
3. At the age of seven she lived and studied with a tutor.
4. Anne Sullivan, her tutor, became a friend and taught Helen some language.
5. Anne started with Helen's sense of touch.

6. Anne tapped and spelled letters on Helen's hand.
7. Helen drank some water and felt Anne's taps on her hand at the same time.
8. The taps stood for the water.
9. In three years, Helen learned the alphabet and made progress in reading.
10. She finally learned enough to go to college.

4c A compound sentence is made up of two or more simple sentences.

Often the sentences are joined by the conjunctions *and, but, or, for,* or *nor.*

EXAMPLES The women marched faster. The old man nearly had to run.
[These two simple sentences may be joined by a comma and the conjunction *and.* Together, they make a compound sentence.]

The women marched faster, *and* the old man nearly had to run.

EXERCISE 7 Some of the following ten sentences are compound sentences. Others are simple sentences. On a sheet of paper write only the compound sentences.

1. Air most often carries sounds to the human ear, but water also carries sound.
2. The ear can hear sound waves.
3. Sound is made up of tiny waves of pressure.
4. These waves strike the ear and cause a little bone to move.

5. The bone moves against nerves in the ear, and the nerves carry a message to the brain.
6. Many animals make sounds humans cannot hear, but other animals can hear those sounds.
7. Some animals, such as bats, use sound waves to help them fly in the dark.
8. They can hear notes that are very high pitched.
9. Bats make screeching sounds, and then they listen for echoes.
10. They can hear the echoes and "see" objects with their ears.

Purposes of Sentences

4d   Sentences are used for four different purposes.

(1) A sentence may declare a fact, an opinion, or a feeling.

This kind of sentence is called a *declarative sentence.*

EXAMPLES   Here comes the streetsweeper.
I like fresh figs.

A declarative sentence ends with a period(.).

(2) A sentence may ask a question.

This kind of a sentence is called an *interrogative sentence.*

EXAMPLES   Can you hear me?
When are you going to get up?

An interrogative sentence ends with a question mark (**?**).

(3)   **A sentence may request or order something.**

This kind of sentence is called an *imperative sentence.*

EXAMPLES   Bring me that can of beans.
Be here at 8:30 tomorrow morning.

An imperative sentence usually ends with a period (**.**), although it may sometimes end with an exclamation mark (**!**).

(4)   **A sentence may express surprise or shock.**

This kind of sentence is called an *exclamatory sentence.*

EXAMPLES   How stupid this is!
He drove the car right into the pole!

An exclamatory sentence ends with an exclamation mark (**!**).

EXERCISE 8   Following are ten sentences without end punctuation. Copy each sentence and add the correct end punctuation. After each sentence, write *D* if it is a declarative sentence, *I* if it is an interrogative sentence, *Imp* if it is an imperative sentence, and *E* if it is an exclamatory sentence.

EXAMPLE   The street is very crowded.

The street is very crowded. D

1. Why are these people marching
2. They seem so angry
3. What a pity they are not happy
4. Many of them are carrying signs
5. Can you read what the signs say
6. Some of them have a big word written in red
7. Help
8. Another person is carrying a small sign
9. What does it say
10. Bring home our people

Completers

Every sentence must contain at least one subject and one verb. Often the complete predicate will contain another important word. This kind of word is called a *completer* because it completes or makes clear what the subject and verb are telling about. Completers may be either *objects* or *subject completers*.

4e **The direct object of a sentence receives the action of the verb.**

EXAMPLE Terry hit the ball.
[The ball receives the action of the verb *hit*.]

EXERCISE 9 Number a sheet of paper from 1 to 6. Write the direct object for each sentence.

EXAMPLE Rosa ate the meat.

meat

1. Bill Dias opened his eyes wide.
2. Then he lifted his lunch box from the fence post.
3. He opened the lid.
4. Bill saw a jar of pickles.
5. From inside the jar he plucked a green pickle.
6. He quickly popped the pickle into his mouth!

Hint: Here are the steps to find the direct object of a sentence:

1. Find the verb. (*hit*)
2. Ask: Who or what hit?
   Answer: *Terry*. Terry is the subject.
3. Ask: Who or what did Terry hit?
   Answer: *ball*. Ball is the object.

4f   The subject completer follows the linking verb and completes the meaning of the sentence. See Linking Verb, p. 265

The subject completer may be a noun or pronoun, an adjective, or an adverb.

EXAMPLES   Sarah seems friendly.
[The adjective *friendly* completes the meaning of the sentence by telling how Sarah seems.]

Mr. Williams is my teacher.
[The noun *teacher* completes the meaning of the sentence by telling who Mr. Williams is.]

The crowd looked angry.
[The adverb *angry* tells how the crowd looked.]

Hint: Here are the steps to follow to find the subject completer:

1. Find the linking verb. In the first example above, the verb is *seems*.
2. Find the subject. Ask "Who or what is?"
   The answer, *Sarah,* is the subject.
3. Then ask, "Sarah seems what?"
   The answer is *friendly. Friendly* is the subject completer.

EXERCISE 10   Following are five sentences. Number your paper from 1 to 5. Next to each number, write the subject completer.

1. My father is the driver.
2. He is usually happy.
3. The winner was Manny.
4. He looked tired.
5. That may be him now.

Sentence Patterns

The basic parts of sentences may be put together in different patterns. The most common sentence patterns are shown here.

Sentence pattern 1:   SUBJECT—VERB (S-V)

EXAMPLES
$\overset{S}{Eddie} \overset{V}{slept.}$

$\overset{S}{The\ bark}$ of the dog $\overset{V}{echoed}$ in the street.

$\overset{S}{Eddie} \overset{V}{jumped.}$

EXERCISE 11 Number a sheet of paper from 1 to 8. Skip a space between each number. Find the subject-verb (S-V) pattern in each of the following eight sentences. After each number, write the simple subject and the verb in the sentence. Write *S* over the subject and *V* over the verb.

EXAMPLE   Raindrops rattled against the window.

Raindrops rattled

1. Most owls sleep in the daytime.
2. They nest in tall trees or barns.
3. At night the owls hunt for mice.
4. An owl's hooting sounds scary.
5. Scared mice run away.
6. But farmers listen eagerly.
7. They understand.
8. They sleep more easily with an owl nearby.

Sentence pattern 2:   SUBJECT—VERB—OBJECT (S-V-O)

EXAMPLES
$\overset{S}{Jeanie} \overset{V}{opened}$ the $\overset{O}{door.}$
[*Door* receives the action of the verb. It is the thing acted upon.]

<pre>
         S   V   O
</pre>
The man dropped the bundle.
[*Bundle* is what the man dropped.]

<pre>
      S   V   O
</pre>
Jeanie slammed the door.
[*Door* is what Jeanie slammed.]

EXERCISE 12 Rewrite the following sentences on your paper. Put *S* over the simple subject, *V* over the verb, and *O* over the object.

EXAMPLE Jeanie grabbed the bundle.

Jeanie grabbed the bundle.

1. Debbie brought her scissors.
2. Jeanie cut the string.
3. Then she unwrapped the brown paper.
4. Inside they discovered two blouses.
5. A plastic wrapper covered each blouse.
6. One girl carefully wrapped them again.
7. The other tied the bundle tightly.
8. Then they quietly placed it on their doorstep.
9. Debbie called the laundry.
10. The next day they saw no bundle.

Sentence pattern 3:   SUBJECT—LINKING VERB—SUBJECT COMPLETER (S-LV-SC)

<pre>
                    S   LV SC
</pre>
EXAMPLES **Mrs. Tracy is sad.**
<pre>
          S   LV   SC
</pre>
Her dog appears dead.
<pre>
        S LV   SC
</pre>
But he is a healthy dog.
<pre>
      S   LV   SC
</pre>
He looks alive.

EXERCISE 13 Rewrite the following sentences on your paper. Put *S* over the simple subject, *LV* over the verb, and *SC* over the subject completer.

EXAMPLE Today Wimpy looks peppy.

Today Wimpy looks peppy.
(S over Wimpy, LV over looks, SC over peppy)

1. His eyes are bright.
2. His ears stand straight.
3. His tail is bushy.
4. His fur is glossy.
5. He is a lively squirrel.
6. His family is lucky.

EXERCISE 14 Copy each of the following sentences on a sheet of paper. Skip a line between each sentence. Put *S* over the simple subject, and *V* or *LV* over the verb. If the sentence has an object, put *O* over it. If the sentence has a subject completer, put *SC* over it.

EXAMPLES Charley made his bed.

Charley made his bed.
(S over Charley, V over made, O over bed)

This morning he looks tired.

This morning he looks tired.
(S over he, LV over looks, SC over tired)

1. Charley Sharp ate a big breakfast.
2. He was hungry.
3. He drank orange juice.
4. His mother cooked sausages.
5. Charley seemed impatient.
6. He wanted buttered toast, too.

7. So Charley consumed five pieces of buttered toast.
8. The toaster grew hot.
9. Afterward Charley looked sleepy.
10. But he felt fine.

SENTENCE PROBLEMS

Writing clear, useful sentences is not always easy. Sometimes you may know what you want to say, but you may have trouble putting your ideas into sentences that others understand. You can make your sentences mean what you want them to, however, if you watch for some common problems.

Sentence Fragments

4g A sentence fragment is an incomplete sentence.

A sentence fragment lacks the parts of a sentence needed to make a complete statement. A fragment may lack a subject or a predicate. Or a fragment may lack both a subject and a predicate.

EXAMPLES   Sang in the treetop and then flew away
[Who or what sang and flew? The fragment does not say.]

The street light here and the one on the corner
[What happened to those lights? The fragment does not say.]

Alive and happy
[Someone might be alive and
happy. But this fragment does not
say it.]

Sometimes a sentence fragment has a subject
and a predicate, but it still needs something to
make it complete.

EXAMPLES   After Bert started the car
           [What happened after Bert started
           the car?]

           Because Sue hates liver
           [What is the result of Sue's hating
           liver?]

The sentence fragment with a subject and a
predicate needs more to explain its meaning. It
needs another statement that is a complete
thought.

EXAMPLE   After Bert started the car, he backed
          it up.
          [*He backed it up* is a complete
          thought. It completes the meaning
          begun but not finished in the
          fragment *After Bert started the
          car.*]

EXERCISE 15   Number a sheet of paper from 1 to
10. The following ten items include some complete
sentences and some fragments. Write *F* after the
number for each fragment. Write *S* after the number of each complete sentence.

EXAMPLE   Rode to the corner

               F

1. Ended up really mad
2. The fish bit at the hook
3. Flopping and splashing
4. A great, silver-sided swimmer
5. Water showered all over us
6. When we got wet
7. But until everyone can clean up
8. We need grease in the pan
9. The head and tail and all the fins
10. Tasty meat

EXERCISE 16   Each of the following items is a fragment because it lacks a subject or a predicate. Rewrite each fragment on your paper to make it a complete sentence.

> EXAMPLE   Fat frogs in this pond
>
> *Fat frogs swim in this pond.*

1. Bees and other insects all through the woods
2. Had landed on a leaf
3. Was chewing the green edge
4. A furry caterpillar with many legs
5. The trunk right up to the top
6. Fell to the ground under the tree
7. Picked it up on a stick
8. Nothing like this in the city
9. Crawled around awhile near the bush
10. Shiny bugs and other creeping or flying things

EXERCISE 17   Following are ten fragments that are incomplete in meaning. Add a complete statement before or after each fragment to make it a complete sentence.

EXAMPLE Until the bus comes.

We will wait here until the bus comes.

Until the bus comes, we will wait here.

1. Before we get on
2. If it is going to the Shopwise Center
3. As we enter
4. By the time we reach the parking lot
5. In case it rains
6. After we have some lunch
7. Only if the sale is still on
8. Whenever you see a good bargain
9. Until we rest our feet
10. Just before we got back

Sometimes a sentence fragment is caused by the incorrect use of capital letters and punctuation. The second one below is a fragment.

EXAMPLE The janitor called us up. Whenever the noise got too loud.

These can be combined into a complete sentence by correcting the capitalization and punctuation.

EXAMPLE The janitor called us up whenever the noise got too loud.

EXERCISE 18 Following are six items that include fragments. Rewrite each numbered item as a complete sentence.

EXAMPLE   Can Jackie wait? Until after
breakfast.

Can Jackie wait until after breakfast?

1. What time was it? When she left.
2. She left about ten. Or before we did.
3. She took the car. And then parked it downtown.
4. It had your gloves on the seat. But not your cap.
5. Your hands will get cold. If she stays away long.
6. But you can keep your head warm. Because you
   have a cap.

EXERCISE 19 Some of the following items are
sentences. Others are fragments. Number your
paper from 1 to 15. Mark each complete sentence *S*.
Rewrite each fragment to make it into a complete
sentence.

EXAMPLES   Neatly folded on the table.

The shirt was neatly folded on the table.

Sue will finish the job. When she
wants it.

Sue will finish the job when she wants it.

1. After the real thing comes along.
2. Until then, I'll wait.
3. That is a friendly idea.
4. After that, I will quit.
5. Because you are angry.
6. Will you please come over?

7. Including Jean and me.
8. After that person left.
9. Until you begin the race.
10. Joan has been very unhappy since Tom left.
11. Insisted that I leave also.
12. Before we start a fight.
13. If it is all right with you.
14. If that ends it, then I will go.
15. Whatever you say.

Run-on Sentences

4h **A run-on sentence is two or more sentences incorrectly joined.**

> EXAMPLE Lennie ran to his room he was
> looking for the quarter.
> or
> Lennie ran to his room, he was
> looking for the quarter.

Most run-on sentences can be corrected by making separate sentences.

> EXAMPLE Lennie ran to his room. He was
> looking for the quarter.

EXERCISE 20 Number a sheet of paper from 1 to 10. Some of the following sentences are run-on sentences. Some are not. Write *R* next to the number of each run-on sentence. Write *S* next to the number of each complete sentence.

> EXAMPLE Lennie Wirtz lives in an apartment
> he goes to Lincoln Junior High.
> *R*

1. Lennie visited a farm two summers ago he could stay only a week.
2. His aunt owns the farm it has more than forty acres.
3. His aunt has a hired man, Tom Hirsch, to help her work the farm.
4. Lennie worked in the fields with his aunt and Tom they planted corn and beans and tomatoes.
5. His aunt showed Lennie how to drive her tractor then he plowed some ground with it.
6. Tom walked behind as Lennie and his aunt sat in the tractor's seat.
7. Lennie had to steer in straight rows and not go too fast.
8. Tom said Lennie learned fast, he would make a good farmer.
9. Lennie asked his aunt if he could come and live with her and help work on the farm.
10. His aunt said he might like the country better than the city but he had to live in the city he had to go to school.

Hint: To check your writing for run-on sentences, read each sentence out loud with feeling. The tones and pauses of your voice are marked in writing by punctuation and capitalization. Whenever the capitalization and punctuation do not match your voice, look for a run-on sentence.

EXERCISE 21 The following eight sentences are run-on sentences. Rewrite each one on your paper to correct the run-on sentence.

EXAMPLE A pioneer family settled in a dense forest they had made a clearing there for their cabin.

A pioneer family settled in a dense forest. They had made a clearing there for their cabin.

1. A Native American family lived in the forest they were friendly.
2. In the pioneer family was a young girl she made friends with a girl in the other family.
3. One fall day the two girls were playing in an open part of the forest the weather turned cold.
4. The sky clouded over a wind came up it looked as if it would snow.
5. The Native American girl wanted to rejoin her family the pioneer girl wanted to play longer.
6. It began to snow then it got dark.
7. The pioneer girl could not see her way to her home the Native American girl led her safely to her own family.
8. Later the snow stopped the pioneer family was happy the young girl had saved their child.

REVIEW EXERCISE A Subjects and Predicates

Write the following sentences on your paper. Put *S* over the simple subject and *V* over the verb.

EXAMPLE Helicopters fly over traffic.

Helicopters fly over traffic.

1. They can travel low with ease.
2. Their turning radius is small.
3. A pilot can see almost straight down.
4. Their speed varies from zero to over one hundred knots.
5. Pilots say good things about their usefulness.
6. Helicopters can hover over one place.
7. They can even fly backwards.
8. They can land almost anywhere.

REVIEW EXERCISE B   Compound Sentences

Here are pairs of simple sentences. Combine each pair into a compound sentence. Write the compound sentence on your paper.

EXAMPLE   Traffic problems are severe.
Helicopters help to ease them.

Traffic problems are severe, but helicopters help to ease them.

1. Car drivers on crowded highways are at a disadvantage. They cannot see far in front.
2. A traffic jam may be ahead. A driver cannot tell about the trouble.
3. A driver who can see a long distance ahead can turn off a highway. A driver can possibly change lanes.
4. Helicopters cannot help the driver. The pilot can radio information about highway trouble.
5. Helicopters aid traffic. They report what drivers cannot know.

REVIEW EXERCISE C   Purposes of Sentences

On a sheet of paper, write two examples each of a declarative sentence, an interrogative sentence, an imperative sentence, and an exclamatory sentence.

REVIEW EXERCISE D   Parts of a Sentence

At the end of each of the following sentences, in parentheses, is the term *subject, verb, object,* or *subject completer.* Number a sheet of paper from 1 to 8. Next to each number, write the word asked for in the parentheses.

EXAMPLE   Vic gave his glove to Lucie. (object)

glove

1. Lucie gladly took Vic's glove. (verb)
2. It was big on her hand. (subject completer)
3. However, she kept her hand in it. (subject)
4. Vic threw a ball. (object)
5. Lucie caught it easily. (verb)
6. She threw it back hard. (subject)
7. Vic's hand was bare. (subject completer)
8. The ball hurt his hand. (object)

REVIEW EXERCISE E   Sentence Problems

Four of the following word groups are fragments. Four are run-on sentences. On a sheet of paper, rewrite each word group to make it either one or two complete sentences.

EXAMPLE   With half the day gone.

With half the day gone, it was important to hurry.

1. Building a bridge.
2. He had put up the long poles the boards were stretched between those.
3. The boards seemed uneven they might catch a wheel of a cart crossing the bridge.
4. Wheels in the cracks.
5. Would damage or destroy a cart.
6. It was necessary to keep the boards together carts would then be safe.
7. Again and again moved the boards so that they were tight.
8. The first cart passed over the bridge everything held together.

UNIT TWO

COMPOSITION

Paragraphs
Guidelines for Writing

CHAPTER

5

PARAGRAPHS

Often you will want to write more about someone or something than will fit in a single sentence. You may use three or four or even more sentences to tell what you want someone else to know. When you use sentences to tell about a single idea, you arrange them together in a *paragraph*. If you want to tell about several important ideas, you will have to write several paragraphs.

Usually a writer shows the reader where a new idea begins by indenting the first word of each paragraph. Indenting means the first word begins a few spaces from the left-hand margin, as the word *Usually* does in this paragraph.

DEVELOPING PARAGRAPHS

5a A paragraph is a series of sentences that tells about a single idea, description, or action.

Read the following paragraph and look for the main idea.

The continent of Antarctica is about twice the size of the United States, yet life can hardly exist there. So cold and lifeless is this land that it holds more ice than can be found in the rest of the world. No tree or bush or blade of grass grows there. Nothing but bits of moss show in the summer. Even the seals, the penguins, and the other birds living near the coast must get their food from the sea.

If you read this paragraph carefully, you probably found its main idea, or *topic: Antarctica is huge, but it is nearly lifeless.* All of the sentences in this paragraph tell about that one topic.

5b State the main idea of a paragraph in a topic sentence.

Nearly every good paragraph states its main idea in a sentence. This sentence is called the *topic sentence.* The topic sentence is often the first sentence of a paragraph. A paragraph without a topic sentence is usually a weak paragraph.

EXAMPLE

Nearly all homes have electric lights. Many homes use electricity for cooking. Some use it for heating. Electricity powers home appliances, from the refrigerator to power tools.

The reader cannot be sure what the paragraph is about. Is it about electric lights? Or is it about electric heating? Maybe it is about appliances.

The same paragraph with a topic sentence added is stronger.

EXAMPLE

Electricity has become the most important source of power in American homes. Nearly all homes have electric lights. Many homes use electricity for cooking. Some use it for heating. Electricity powers most home appliances, from the refrigerator to power tools.

EXERCISE 1 Number a sheet of paper 1, 2, and 3 to stand for the following paragraphs. Each of the three paragraphs has no topic sentence. Six possible topic sentences are listed at the end of the exercise. Choose the best topic sentence for each paragraph and write it next to the number for that paragraph.

1. (Topic sentence missing) Accidents often happen at crosswalks because a pedestrian steps into the street against a red light. Or a pedestrian may forget to look in all directions before leaving the sidewalk. Crossing on foot in the middle of a block is also dangerous. Walking on a country road where there is no sidewalk can be a problem. There, it is important to walk facing the oncoming traffic.

2. (Topic sentence missing) A whale breathes air, just as other mammals do. Its blood is warm and carries oxygen from its lungs to other parts of the body. The newborn whale lives on its mother's milk until it is old enough to find food in the ocean.

3. (Topic sentence missing) One of the best examples is skiing. Skiers let gravity pull them

down a slope. Surfing, as well, makes use of gravity. The surfer slides down the top or side of a wave. It is gravity that does the pulling. This force also acts in sky diving, the most daring kind of sport. Sky divers let gravity pull them toward the earth. They open their parachutes in time to slow their fall and land safely.

TOPIC SENTENCES

Whales, unlike fish, are true mammals.
Skiing, surfing, and sky diving are all alike.
Walking is good for one's health.
Whales need protection.
Some sports would not work without gravity.
Pedestrians need to remember that safety depends on them.

5c   Make every sentence in a paragraph say something about the topic.

The following paragraph begins with a topic sentence: *The room was a mess.* This is the main idea of the paragraph. Every other sentence tells something about the messy room.

The room was a mess. Chairs were out of place. The center rug was partly rolled up. There were crumbs and stains on the furniture and rugs. Three paper plates with bits of old food still sat on the table. An empty soda bottle lay on its side under the couch. A game board was on the floor. Its cards and pieces were scattered about.

In the next paragraph, the topic sentence again comes first. All the other sentences say something about the topic.

The inning was a disaster for us. Our pitcher, Judy Baum, walked the first three players she faced. The next batter bunted. Judy and Tim, our catcher, both went for the ball and hit head on! As they sat rubbing their heads, two runs scored. Then Judy walked two more batters, forcing in a run. Coach Witt looked mad. Judy hit the next batter with her first pitch. That forced in another run. The next pitch she threw was hit for a home run. Eight runs scored in that inning. We thought we had lost the game for sure.

EXERCISE 2   Number a sheet of paper from 1 to 3. One of the sentences in each of the following three paragraphs does not belong. Write the sentence next to the number of the paragraph.

EXAMPLE

The party was filled with activities. At six o'clock we went on a scavenger hunt, asking neighborhood people for all kinds of strange things. At eight o'clock we went on a hay ride out to the lake. At the lake we built a bonfire and had a cookout. Amy's dad had car trouble. When we had finished eating and cleaning up, we sat in our sleeping bags by the fire, roasted marshmallows, and told ghost stories until after midnight.

Amy's dad had car trouble.

This sentence has nothing to do with the topic that the party was filled with activities.

1. Biology is the study of life. Many people spend their lives as biologists. They study life on land, in the air, and in the water. They study animal life and vegetable life. I like to study mathematics, too.

2. The Monarch butterfly is an amazing insect. It weighs only a little more than a paper clip. Its full life, including its time as a caterpillar, lasts just over a year. Yet during that lifetime, it makes a round-trip journey of over 9,000 miles. Few people walk that far in a year. It travels from Mexico to New England and back again.

3. Soccer is a difficult sport. A player must be able to run steadily without rest. Sometimes a player must hit the ball with his or her head. Players must be willing to bang into and be banged into by others. Some countries have professional soccer teams. Players must put up with aching feet and sore leg muscles.

5d Develop a paragraph with details and examples.

Notice in the next paragraph that the sentences following the topic sentence give details supporting the main idea.

Once a year a snake sheds its skin. It begins the process by rubbing its head against rough objects. This breaks the old skin around the jaws and eyes. Next it crawls forward. If the broken edge of the skin catches on dried grass or a rock, the snake slides ahead. If not, it rubs against other objects. As the snake rubs and slides, the skin slowly peels from the snake's body like the long finger of a glove. Within a half hour the snake is free. Its skin, like clear tissue paper, lies inside out on the ground.

In the next paragraph, the topic is developed with examples.

Different breeds of horses have different characteristics. The Tennessee Walking Horse, for example, has a smooth, gliding gait that keeps the rider comfortable for hours. The Standardbred trots or paces swiftly without breaking into a gallop. The Appaloosa has a strong, muscular body. Cowboys often use this kind of horse. The Arabian has a dark skin that helps it stand the heat of the desert sun. The Shetland pony has a thick, woolly coat to survive the bitter climate of the Shetland Isles.

EXERCISE 3   Here 'are four possible topic sentences. Fill in the blanks for yourself. Then select one topic sentence and write a paragraph of five or more sentences about the main idea. Make each of your sentences supply a new detail or an example to support the topic sentence you select.

1. My _____ is filled with interesting things.
2. _____ is an exciting game.
3. _____ was an interesting (or dull) movie (or television show).
4. _____ was the hardest job I ever did.

5e   A paragraph may be organized by time.

A paragraph arranged by time usually describes events in the order they occur.

EXAMPLES

Yesterday everything went from bad to worse. I woke up with a head cold. When I got out of bed, I stepped on my little brother's model car. I was so mad I kicked it and almost broke a big toe. Then when I tried to get the car out from under the bed, I banged my head on the bed frame. That was only the beginning of my day. From then on, everything went downhill.

Making pancakes is easy. First, break an egg into an empty bowl. Add about a cup of milk and a tablespoon or so of salad oil. Mix those ingredients well. Then add enough sifted flour to make the batter slightly thick. Probably about a cup and a half of flour will do. Add a teaspoon of baking powder. When you have finished mixing the batter, heat a lightly greased frying pan at medium heat. Spoon out two or three cakes. Watch until bubbles form, pop, and begin to leave dry holes. Then turn the pancakes over. Let them cook another minute or two. Remove them. Put them on a plate. Butter them or add syrup. Yummy!

EXERCISE 4   The following paragraph is scrambled. Each numbered sentence after number 1 is out of order. Write down the sentence numbers in correct order on a sheet of paper to show how the sentences should be written. Look for word clues that may help you discover the time order of the paragraph.

1. Playing Rummy is easy. 2. Finally, the player on the left of the dealer lays down the first card. 3. To begin, the dealer deals out seven cards to each player. 4. Then each player puts his or her cards into order. 5. Next, the dealer puts down the deck and turns the top card over.

EXERCISE 5   Following are a topic sentence and some uncompleted sentences. Copy this paragraph on a sheet of paper. Fill in the blanks with your own words. Keep in mind the order of events.

EXAMPLE
   English   class   was   hard   today.   First,
_____ . After   that, _____ .
Then _____ . Finally, _____ .

*English class was hard today. First,
we had a spelling test. After that, we
had a quiz on the story we were
supposed to read for homework. Then
we reviewed parts of speech. Finally,
we had a quiz on them.*

   Last Wednesday was the best day of the year. It began _____ . After that, _____ . Then _____ . And to top the day off, _____ .

5f   A paragraph may be organized by space.

A paragraph arranged by space usually describes an object or a scene. You may begin by describing the front of something. Then describe the middle and the back of it. You may also describe something from the left to the right or from inside to outside. It is important to organize a space-order paragraph in a way that will be clear for the reader to understand.

EXAMPLE

This is what one finds on the "head" side of a penny. At the top are the words *IN GOD WE TRUST* in capital letters. In the middle is the familiar face of Abraham Lincoln. Under his chin is the date the coin was minted and the abbreviation of the place where it was minted. To the left of Lincoln's face is the word *LIBERTY*.

EXERCISE 6 Select two of the following objects. Write a paragraph organized by space. Write five or more sentences about each of the objects you select.

1. The room you are sitting in, moving from your left to your right
2. A dollar bill
3. A television set
4. A car
5. A picture on the front page of a newspaper

5g A paragraph is used to show the words of a new speaker.

Indent the beginning of a quotation. The exact words of a new speaker belong in a paragraph.

EXAMPLE

"Try a front wheelie!" called Donnie, as Janis rolled by.

"I can't, " she answered. But she moved her weight forward toward the tip of the skateboard.

"Put both feet together," shouted Donnie, running now to stay near her.

With her hair flying and her arms balancing like the wings of a soaring bird, Janis carefully pressed forward. The back of the skateboard tipped up an inch or two.

"That's it! You've got it!" Donnie screamed.

"Yeah," breathed Janis. She allowed a wide smile to spread across her mouth.

REVIEW EXERCISE A   Topic Sentences

Following are five topics of paragraphs. On a piece of paper write a topic sentence for each. Plan each sentence to be the first one in a paragraph.

1. A funny valentine card.
2. Breakfast toast
3. A skateboard stunt
4. The best birthday gift
5. Midnight

REVIEW EXERCISE B   Developing by Details

Choose two paragraph topics from Review Exercise A. Make a list of at least three details you would include in each of the two paragraphs.

REVIEW EXERCISE C Writing a Paragraph

Write a short paragraph. Use a topic sentence you wrote for Review Exercise A. Include the details you wrote for Review Exercise B.

GUIDELINES FOR WRITING

Learning to write a paragraph is the first step in learning to write a *composition*. A composition is usually made up of at least several paragraphs. Each of the paragraphs tells about a single topic. The paragraphs put the ideas together to tell about a larger topic. When you organize sentences into a paragraph, you are taking an important step toward writing a successful composition.

CHOOSING YOUR TOPIC AND YOUR AUDIENCE

6a Write first about what you know.

When you are planning what to write about, choose a topic that you know well. Of course, you know yourself best of all. You might want to begin writing about something that happened to you. You can recall experiences that made you feel good, such as a birthday, a favorite meal, or the most exciting day of your life. You may also remember experiences that made you feel bad, such as a fight, or being sick, or being embarrassed. These things you know well.

You may know something else well because you have taken the time to learn about it. Perhaps you have a hobby. Maybe you are good at growing plants. Or you have some other skill. Perhaps you have read many books about a topic, such as heroes of the Old West or dinosaurs. You may know a topic well because you have had experience taking part in it, such as a sport like football or soccer.

Whenever you are trying to decide what to write about, remember to choose a topic that you know well. Even if you think you have little knowledge about a topic, you can look it up in books. You can read about it.

EXERCISE 1 Choose one of the following topics you know about. Remember the events that happened to you. Make a list of the events in the order they happened.

1. My best meal
2. When I was really sick
3. The first money I ever earned
4. My worst fight
5. The best day of my life
6. My last birthday
7. My first day of school

8. The day we moved
9. Summer camp
10. A topic of your choice

EXERCISE 2 Write a short composition of one paragraph telling of an experience you had. Use the topic you chose in Exercise 1 or choose another similar topic.

6b Write first to someone you know.

Writing is somewhat like talking. Both are means of sharing ideas with someone else. When you talk, you express yourself to someone. When you write, think of someone else you are writing to. This will help you to remember to make your thoughts clear to another person, your *audience.*

The person you choose to write to should be someone who does not know all about your topic. If you choose an experience that happened with members of your family, do not write to them. You might choose instead to write to a grandparent who was absent. Or you might write to a friend. The person you write to should find something new in your writing.

If you cannot think of anyone to write to, turn to yourself. Writing to yourself is like writing a private diary. Maybe you have kept a diary already. You know what fun it can be to read over what you have written. Writing a composition to yourself is very much like writing in a diary.

EXERCISE 3 List the names of four people you might write to. Two of them should be about your age. Two should be adults. At least one adult should not be a member of your family.

6c Choose a topic to suit your audience.

You will find it most helpful to write about what you know to someone you know. However, not all the topics that you know well will be interesting to everyone you know. An older relative, such as your grandmother, would probably be more interested in how you spent your spring vacation than in the worst fight you ever had. Your best friend would probably be more interested in how you like the subjects you are taking in school than a visit with a relative.

When you are choosing your topic, be sure to choose one that will interest your audience.

EXERCISE 4   Following are eight topics that you might write about. Some topics you might write about in a letter to an adult, such as someone in your family. Other topics you would write only in your diary or to a close friend your age. Number a sheet of paper from 1 to 8. Next to each number put *A* if you would write about the topic only to an adult. Put *D* if you would write about the topic only in your diary.

1. Unusual weather
2. A minor accident in your home
3. A flood near you
4. A fight you had with a close friend or relative
5. A vacation trip you took
6. A new song by your favorite singer or musical group

7. A movie you have just seen

8. A private note from someone you like very much

EXERCISE 5   Choose a topic from the list in Exercise 4. Or choose another topic that is similar. Choose an audience from your list in Exercise 3. Write a short composition of one paragraph about the topic to the audience you have chosen.

ORGANIZING YOUR WRITING

When you write to someone, you try to get your ideas across. That is, you try to communicate. To be successful, communication depends upon choosing words and phrases carefully. It depends upon writing sentences that mean what you intend. It depends, also, upon planning and organizing what you write.

6d Limit the topic you choose to write about.

As soon as you have decided what topic you would like to write about, it is a good idea to *limit* it, or make it smaller. A topic of interest to you may be too big to write about in just one paragraph or even several paragraphs. Suppose, for example, you are greatly interested in horses. You plan to write something about them. If you choose the topic *horses,* you might have to write a large book to tell all you know about horses. Instead, it's best to limit the topic. Tell about just one kind of horse. Or tell just one special thing about horses. This way, you will be able to write about your topic more easily.

Here are some examples of topics that have been limited so they are easier to write about.

TOPIC	LIMITED TOPIC
Fishing	Fishing at Lake George
	or
	The best bait for bass
	or
	The fun of fly fishing
How to spend free time	Books are better than TV
	or
	A sport for myself
Pets	Our funny family dog
	or
	The best food for a pet cat

EXERCISE 6 The following list contains five large topics and five limited ones. Write the topics on your paper in two columns. Head one column *broad topics*. Head the other column *limited topics*.

Dogs as pets
The best kind of music
  for listening
The best science fiction
  book
How to teach a dog
  a trick

Conservation
Camping
Inventions of this
  century
The history of music
A place not to camp
Saving water at home

6e Relate events in the order they happened.

Events usually happen over a period of time instead of all at once. When writing about events, keep them in the right order in time.

Suppose you choose to write to a relative or friend about the best meal you ever had. It is quite easy to keep the events in order. An event would be the eating of each dish of food.

EXERCISE 7   Following are some possible dishes in a special meal. Eating each one is a kind of event. On a sheet of paper write the dishes in the order you would eat them. You may change some of the dishes if you like or add some new ones. Be sure to list them in order.

steak	pizza slices
tomato juice	fresh fruitcup
potatoes	dessert
vegetable	hot rolls

6f   Tell where events happened.

Events you have experienced happened some-where. The place or setting of events needs to be included in your writing. This helps your reader "see" what you are writing about. Think about where you had your experience. Add that information to your writing.

Did you eat your best meal in a restaurant? Was it at home? Was it a picnic outdoors? Or did you eat at a friend's? What were the surroundings like where you had your meal? The answers to questions like these help locate your experience for your reader.

Events happen someplace. Let your reader know *where* you had your experience.

EXERCISE 8 Write a short composition of one paragraph describing a place where something interesting happened to you. Write it to an audience that has not seen the place. In your writing, help your audience "see" the place you describe.

CHOOSING YOUR WORDS

6g **Use words and phrases that appeal to the senses.**

One good way to describe someone or something is to use words that appeal to the senses. Keep in mind that your reader probably has the same five senses you have. These are the senses of sight, hearing, touch, taste, and smell.

Following are some words that appeal to each of the five senses.

SIGHT	HEARING	TOUCH	TASTE	SMELL
red	squeaky	rough	bitter	perfume
crooked	sniffle	wrinkled	sugary	lemony
cloudy	rattle	silken	peppery	dank

Words like these help to make writing more effective. They make it possible for the reader to appreciate the experience you are writing about. What you tell about becomes more special.

EXERCISE 9 The following sentences need descriptive words in the blanks. Five words that appeal to the senses are listed below the sentences. Number a sheet of paper from 1 to 5. Choose a word from the list below to fit in the blank in each sentence. Write the word next to the number for the sentence.

1. The hot frying pan sent up a smell of _____ grease.
2. When I picked up the _____ ice cube, it immediately fell to the floor.
3. I held the _____ jellybean in the corner of my mouth.
4. The _____ edge of the leaf scratched her arm.
5. The milk had turned the breakfast cereal into a _____ pile.

sugary   burnt   slippery
mushy   prickly

Suppose you decide to write about an accident you had on your old bicycle. You know the bicycle's features. However, your reader does not know them. Use words that will help your reader see, hear, and even feel the bicycle. Here are some words you might use to make the parts come alive:

chipped paint   *bent* fenders
squeaky wheels   *clanking* chain

EXERCISE 10   In Column A is a list of parts of a bicycle. In Column B are words that describe what those parts look and sound like. Copy the words in Column A on your paper. Choose a word from Column B to describe each part in Column A. Write that word next to the part it describes.

EXAMPLE   *wheel, squeaky*

COLUMN A   COLUMN B
1. wheel   bent
2. seat   chipped

CHOOSING YOUR WORDS 117

3. pedal   dented
4. chain   smashed
5. chainguard   clanking
6. fender   grinding
7. tire   muddy
8. handlebars   cracked
                  wobbly
                  banging
                  squeaky

EXERCISE 11 Write a paragraph of at least five sentences describing an old bicycle. Use words that describe how it looks and how it sounds. If you have the opportunity, read your paragraph aloud to others. Can they picture what you have described?

EXERCISE 12 Choose some other object familiar to you. Write a paragraph describing it. Have someone else read your description. See if your reader can tell what you have described.

6h Use comparisons in your descriptions.

Another way to help your reader is to compare the things you write about with other things. Your reader can then understand more fully what you are describing. Comparisons often use the word *like* or the word *as*.

EXAMPLES   The dog's tongue was *like wet sandpaper*.
            The cloud looked *like a giant white horse*.
            The crust of the stale roll was *as hard as a football helmet*.

EXERCISE 13 Following are two lists. List A contains objects or their features. List B contains comparisons. Number a sheet of paper from 1 to 6. Next to each number, write the item from List A. Next to it write the best comparison from List B. The first one is done for you as an example.

EXAMPLE *contented as a well-fed cat*

LIST A

1. contented
2. a long leaf
3. slippery
4. TV antennas in a row
5. a thin old man asleep
6. an excited crowd

LIST B

as an oily ball-bearing
like a fallen dead tree
as a well-fed cat
like buzzing bees
like a hedge without leaves
like a green spearhead

EXERCISE 14 The things or features in the following list need comparisons to make them come alive. Write five of these items on a sheet of paper and add comparisons of your own.

EXAMPLE a roar

a roar like a jet engine

1. a fire
2. a shriek
3. soft
4. a groan
5. sunlight

6. a sheet of steel
7. rain
8. grass
9. a rubber ball
10. sand

EXERCISE 15 Choose one of the following topics. On a sheet of paper write a composition of at least two paragraphs. Include some comparisons in your writing to help the reader share your experience.

1. My worst accident
2. The dumbest thing I ever did
3. The day I made my mother (father, brother, sister, best friend) happy.
4. The day I made my mother (father, brother, sister, best friend) angry.
5. The time I got lost
6. The smartest thing I ever did

6i Be specific by adding details or examples.

Everybody has ideas that are based on opinions or feelings. Often you may hear people say things like this:

"I like to watch baseball on television."
"McGrundy's hamburgers are the best."
"I can't stand anyone who puts on a lot of perfume."
"That must be the worst book ever written."

Maybe you have said some of the same kinds of things. The trouble with these statements is that they are not supported by specific information. Details and examples help explain what the statement means or why the person has that opinion or feeling.

When you express an idea, you can increase its value by adding specific information in the form of details and examples. This is particularly true in your own writing.

EXAMPLES

STATEMENT	SPECIFIC INFORMATION
1. Movies seem better to see in a theater than on TV at home.	Larger screen, clearer picture, better sound, no commercials.

2. Roses always make   Perfect shape of petals,
   me feel a sense of   delicate perfume, frag-
   wonder.   ile blossoms, glorious
                              colors.

3. The old mill is a   Built of hardcut stone,
   good example of   thatched roof, wooden
   eighteenth-century   wheel.
   architecture.

When you plan to write about an idea, opinion, or feeling, it is best to begin by writing a topic sentence. Then list the information that supports your statement. Include it in your composition.

EXERCISE 16 Following are statements anyone might make. Choose one statement. Fill in the information in parentheses with what you know. Write the completed statement on a sheet of paper. Think of as many supporting details as you can and write these down under your statement.

1. *(name of a kind of car)* is the best car for the money.
2. *(name of a store)* is the best place to buy *(name of something)*.
3. *(name of an intersection)* is the most dangerous place in the area.
4. *(name of a person)* is the best-dressed person in school.
5. *(name of a day of the week)* is the best day of the week.

EXERCISE 17 Write about your topic from Exercise 16. Use the supporting information you have listed to write a brief composition of at least one paragraph. Remember to state your opinion or feel-

ing at the start. Then support this topic sentence
with the details and examples you have listed.

WRITING LETTERS AND NOTES

Writing a letter or an important note is a kind
of composition. You must think ahead what you
want to communicate. You must suit your writing
to your reader. You must remember to keep your
points in order.

You may write a letter to a relative. Or you
may write to a friend your own age. You may even
write to someone you don't know well. In every
case, you need to plan your letter carefully. You
also need to write it with care.

**6j   Write friendly letters in content and form
pleasing to the receiver.**

The friendly letter is the name of a type of letter. It is almost any letter that is not a business
letter. A business letter is formal. A friendly letter
is informal.

However, an informal friendly letter should
not be written carelessly. Since a friend is someone
you respect, a friendly letter should show respect.
Its content should be clear.

The best friendly letter is one that shows you
at your best as a friendly person. It is a pleasure to
receive and read.

Here are a few steps to follow in writing a good
friendly letter.

1. Use stationery that is neat. Use ink, not pencil. A typewriter is all right, but sign your name in ink.
2. Think ahead of the points you want to make. If necessary, write them down on a separate piece of paper. Make your sentences make sense. If you are answering a letter, make sure you touch on each of the main points in it. Answer any questions.
3. Write with your best handwriting. Write evenly across the page, with margins 1-1½ inches at the top and left. Avoid writing words at angles or up and down the sides.
4. If you make a mistake, draw one even line through the error. Then write the correction either above or after the error.
5. Follow the standard form for letters.

4220 Chicago Circle
Gary, Indiana 60673
May 21, 1983

Dear Emma,

Mom and Dad said I could visit you after school! That's the best news. And I have only three more weeks of school. That's the next best news.

I hope we can do lots of swimming. Also, will the Nordniks' horses be around? I love to go riding bareback. I know we're not supposed to run them, but if we walk them down past the trees, then maybe we can get them to trot. That way they won't get too hot, and we can walk them back slowly.

Dad said he'd drive me down the day after school. So unless something goes wrong (I hope it won't), I'll see you the Saturday after school. Let me know if I should bring anything special.

Sincerely,
Daisy

Notice in the friendly letter above that the important information is given in the first paragraph. The next information—and a question—is in the second paragraph. The final information—how Daisy is coming—is in the last paragraph. The information about travel and arrival might have been put in the second paragraph. However, it is the fact that it is included in the letter that is important.

EXERCISE 18 Write a friendly letter to suit one of the following situations. Or write a letter based on a real situation you know.

1. You have just moved to a new town. You write to a friend where you used to live, telling that person about your new home. You also ask what has been happening in your former town.
2. A close friend has moved three weeks before to a new town. You write your friend some of the events of your home area. You also ask for a letter telling about your friend's new experiences.

3. You have been away from home on a vacation with a friend for two weeks. You write a letter home to your family telling them what has been happening.

Once you have written a letter, take care with the envelope. If the envelope is not correctly treated, your letter may not be received. You must write the name and address of both the receiver and yourself on the outside of the envelope. Moreover, you must put on the correct amount of postage. The U.S. Postal Service may not deliver a letter if it has no postage on it.

Here is a model of an envelope that is correctly addressed.

> Linda Wong
> 3140 Clay St., #2
> San Francisco, Ca. 94115
>
>
>   Susan Sias
>   617 Poseyville Road
>   Midland, Michigan 48640

REVISING YOUR WRITING

6k **Revise your writing to improve its effectiveness.**

After you have written a composition, you can improve it by reading it over carefully. Look at the words you have used. Some other words may be more exact in their meaning. Substitute new words where they will improve upon the ones you have.

Do the phrases you have used relate correctly to other parts of the sentence? If not, can you move them to improve your sentence?

Do your sentences say what you want them to? Are they related to each other so that your reader can follow your ideas?

Does each paragraph have a topic sentence that states the main idea clearly? If you have written more than one paragraph, are they in a logical order?

6l Check the mechanics of your writing.

Make your composition as readable as you can. Is your penmanship legible? Have you checked spelling, capitalization, and punctuation?

Refer to the following Composition Checklist. If you can honestly answer yes to all or most of those questions, you have written a successful composition.

COMPOSITION CHECKLIST

1. Do you know enough about your topic?
2. Do you know who your audience is?
3. Does your topic suit your audience?
4. Is your topic limited so that you can deal with it?
5. Have you organized the events according to time and place?
6. Have you used words and phrases that appeal to the five senses of the audience?

7. Have you used comparisons?
8. Have you supported main ideas with specific details and examples?
9. Does each paragraph develop a single idea or event?
10. Are your words, phrases, and sentences doing their best work?
11. Have you left any phrases separated from complete sentences?
12. Have you checked the mechanics to the best of your ability?

REVIEW EXERCISE A   Choosing an Audience

In the column at the left are four topics for composition. In the column at the right are different audiences. On a sheet of paper, write the topics in a column at the left. Next to each topic, write the audience that would be most interested in reading your composition about the topic.

TOPIC	AUDIENCE
An ugly bug I found	A teacher or school
A visit to a favorite rela-	principal
tive's home	A parent
What I like (or dislike)	A friend your age
about English	
What I like (or dislike)	
about milk	

REVIEW EXERCISE B   Limited Topics

Following are possible topics for a composition. Some of them are too large for a short composition

(1-3 paragraphs). Some topics are limited enough for a short composition. On your paper, write the topics that are limited enough to use for a short composition.

> An internal combustion engine
> The value of a hem
> How to conserve energy
> Prehistoric monsters
> Feeding hamsters
> Storm windows in the winter
> My shoes in the year 2000
> The minting of a coin
> Baking cookies
> Money for all countries

REVIEW EXERCISE C Appealing to the Senses

In the following paragraphs you will find twenty words and phrases that appeal to the senses. Each one has a number over it. Across the top of your paper write the five senses, as shown below. Under each sense write the numbers of the words and phrases that appeal to that sense.

SIGHT   SOUND   TOUCH   TASTE   SMELL

I had seen my older sister make chocolate fudge. That gave me the idea I could make some, too. The one day I was alone at home, I tried it.

First I found a large pot. Then I got a box of bit-
1
tersweet chocolate squares and broke them into

tiny pieces into the pot. Some of them broke with a
snap. Others came apart with a muffled sound.
From the refrigerator, I took some pieces of yellow
margarine. They were wrapped in a waxy paper. I
cut some slippery chunks of margarine with a sharp
knife and put them in the pot. Then I got out a
floppy bag half full of sugar and dumped some in
the pot. It poured from the bag like a miniature
waterfall, but with white, dry crystals instead of
clear water. Then I turned on the stove under the
pot.

Soon the margarine and chocolate began to melt.
I stirred the soft pieces. My spoon slid around, but
in some places it rubbed grainy sugar and made a
scratching sound on the pot. As everything began to
melt, the snowy sugar turned dark brown and the
margarine disappeared into a gooey syrup. Bubbles
began to rise in the fudge. They made it look like a
pot-sized pool of hot lava. The sweet smell of melt-
ing chocolate filled the kitchen. Its heavy odor filled
my nostrils.

UNIT THREE

USAGE

Using Parts of Speech
Common Confusions

7

USING PARTS OF SPEECH

Think of every sentence you write as a finely tuned engine. When all of the parts fit together smoothly, the engine does its work. If one of the parts does not fit, however, the engine stops.

The words in a sentence affect the way it works. The noun or pronoun that is the subject, for example, helps you decide what form of verb to use. The type of the verb you choose—action or linking—helps you decide what words are needed following it.

The different parts of a sentence must fit together. They must *agree* with each other if you want to write correct, clear sentences.

AGREEMENT OF SUBJECTS AND VERBS

See Verb, p. 273

Verbs in English have many forms. The correct form of a verb depends partly on how many persons or things are being talked about as the subject of a sentence.

The number of people or things that a verb describes is called just that: *number*. The number may be only one. Or the number may be more than one. One person or thing is called *singular*. More than one is called *plural*.

EXAMPLE

SINGULAR The girl skates over the ice.
PLURAL Three girls skate over the ice.

Most nouns change their forms to show the difference between singular and plural.

See Noun, p. 266

EXAMPLES

SINGULAR toy   watch   drop
PLURAL   toys   watches drops

Only a few nouns do not change form to show a difference between singular and plural. The plural of *deer* is *deer,* for example.

7a A verb must agree with its subject in number.

A noun or pronoun that is the subject of a sentence affects the form of the verb. If the subject is singular, the verb must be singular. If the subject is plural, the verb must be plural.

EXAMPLES Juan speaks clearly.
The rat runs swiftly.
Rats hide in tiny holes.
The students know the answer.

Hint: If the plural noun ends in **s,** the verb usually does not end in **s.**

See Pronoun, p. 270
A pronoun may take the place of the noun subject in a sentence. The verb must agree with this pronoun, just as it does with the noun.

EXAMPLES   *The engine runs* on unleaded gas.
It runs on unleaded gas.

Jane plans to tune the engine tonight.
She plans to tune the engine tonight.

A noun in plural form that is thought of as singular usually takes a singular verb.

EXAMPLES   *The news is* not all bad.
Fifty cents is hardly enough to last a week.

Add the letter **s** or the letters **es** to a regular verb in the present tense if the subject is a single person or thing (third person singular). All other subjects (first and second person singular and plural and third person plural) use only the infinitive form of the verb for the present tense.

EXAMPLES	PRESENT TENSE
	Singular Form
FIRST PERSON	I eat, dance, play
SECOND PERSON	You eat, dance, play
THIRD PERSON	He/she/it eats, dances, plays

Bill/Mary/Fido eats, dances, plays

Plural Form

FIRST PERSON	We eat, dance, play
	Bill and I eat, dance, play
SECOND PERSON	You (all) eat, dance, play
THIRD PERSON	They eat, dance, play
	Bill and Mary eat, dance, play

EXERCISE 1 Number a sheet of paper from 1 to 10. After each number, write down the correct form of the verb from each of the following sentences.

EXAMPLE The girl in the middle of the people (sing/sings) well.

sings

1. Ellen (sing/sings) better than Jodie.
2. They (try/tries) to sing together.
3. But Jodie (seem/seems) to have trouble staying with Ellen.
4. The news today (is/are) very interesting.
5. Jodie (begin/begins) on another note.
6. They (sound/sounds) like two sick cats.
7. Ellen (stop/stops) after a while.
8. She (hear/hears) Jodie's voice.
9. Jodie (keep/keeps) on singing.
10. The rest of us (do/does) not like to listen.

EXERCISE 2 Number a sheet of paper from 1 to 10. Write *S* for a singular subject and verb. Write *P* for a plural subject and verb.

1. dogs howl   6. they jog
2. trains run   7. monkey leaps
3. it puffs   8. wind blows
4. planet turns   9. drops fall
5. stars shine   10. we practice

EXERCISE 3 Number a sheet of paper from 1 to 10. Change each singular subject and verb to the plural. Change each plural subject and verb to the singular.

EXAMPLES papers tear

paper tears

they fly

it flies (or he flies, she flies)

1. ships sail   6. sailor slides
2. storm comes   7. men help
3. waves rise   8. they fall
4. waters splash   9. he swims
5. sailors run   10. it stops

EXERCISE 4 Some of the following sentences contain errors. Some have a singular subject but a plural verb. Others have a plural subject but a singular verb. Rewrite each sentence that has an error in subject-verb agreement and make the necessary corrections.

EXAMPLE Most sea birds eats fish.

Most sea birds eat fish.

1. Sea birds fly for long distances without resting.
2. Albatrosses of the sea soar easily for days.
3. A large albatross follow ships half way across the ocean.
4. Seagulls also makes long trips out to sea.
5. Their long flights over water means they must find food from the ocean.
6. Birds of the sea live mostly on fish.

7b A compound subject is joined by a conjunction and usually takes a plural verb.

Some sentences have two or more subjects. See Sentences, p. 72 Their subjects are often joined by the conjunction *and.* They become the *compound subject.*

EXAMPLES Ned rides a motorbike to school.
[Singular subject and singular verb]

Ollie rides with Ned.
[Singular subject and singular verb]

Ned and Ollie ride a motorbike to school.
[Compound subject and plural verb]

Occasionally the two or more persons or items that make up a compound subject are thought of as being one.

EXAMPLE Burns and Allen is a good name for a comedy team.

EXERCISE 5 Number your paper from 1 to 10. Next to each number write the correct form of the verb given in the parentheses.

> EXAMPLE Whales and dolphins (is/are) not real fish.
>
> *are*

1. Whales and dolphins (swims/swim) like fish.
2. Whales and dolphins (is/are) different from fish.
3. Scientists (calls/call) them mammals.
4. A whale (grows/grow) bigger than a dolphin.
5. A whale (is/are) the largest mammal on earth.
6. Whales and dolphins (hears/hear) sounds we cannot hear.
7. Other mammals (makes/make) their home in the ocean.
8. Seals and otters (is/are) mammals, too.
9. The seal and the otter (lives/live) in water more than on land.
10. Seals and otters (comes/come) out on the shore sometimes.

7c When subjects are joined by the conjunctions *or, nor, either . . . or,* or *neither . . . nor,* the verb agrees in number with the nearer subject.

> EXAMPLES Two side mirrors or one hubcap *was* what he offered me.
> One hubcap or two tire wrenches *were* what I wanted.

EXERCISE 6 Number a sheet of paper from 1 to 5. Write the correct form of the verb next to each number.

EXAMPLE Neither the mashed potatoes nor the meat (looks/look) good.

looks

1. Sliced tomatoes or cottage cheese (comes/come) with the meal.
2. Milk or root beer (is/are) offered.
3. Neither this restaurant nor others in town (gives/give) its customers cloth napkins.
4. Pie or ice cream (is/are) included with the meal.
5. Either cash or a credit card (pays/pay) the bill.

7d **When a group of words comes between the subject and the verb, the verb still agrees with the subject.**

There may be words in a sentence that come between the subject and its verb. You should be careful to make the verb agree with the subject and not with any of these words.

EXAMPLES The *man* with the groceries *is* my uncle.
The *boys* leaning out the window *look* like my cousins.

EXERCISE 7 Number a sheet of paper from 1 to 11. Choose the correct form of the verb in each of the following sentences. Write the verb next to the number.

EXAMPLE The car with the fender dents
(needs/need) new paint.

needs

1. Jobs for the summer (is/are) hard to find.
2. Older people not in school (has/have) a better chance for work.
3. Anybody without work experience (finds/find) it hard to get a job.
4. My neighbors on the street (give/gives) work once in a while.
5. Vic Berger, down the street from us, (gets/get) jobs on weekends.
6. The owner of these new houses (gives/give) him five dollars to pick up trash.
7. The trash lying around his houses (fills/fill) three large cans.
8. The builders, with all their work, (leaves/leave) most of the trash.
9. The work of picking up wood chips and nails (is/are) worth five dollars.
10. Vic, with the help of his brother and sister, (does/do) the job in about two hours.
11. The neighbors, including Mr. Kent, (agree/agrees) that the Berger children are hard workers.

SPECIAL VERB PROBLEMS

See Verbs,
pp. 34–36

Verbs show time by their form. Time in the present is called *present tense*. It is shown by the infinitive form of nearly all verbs. Examples are *borrow, fold,* and *begin.*

Regular Verbs

Regular verbs change form to show past time, or *past tense,* in two ways. These verbs add **d** or **ed** to the infinitive to show that an action happened in the *simple past.* To show another past time, called the *present perfect,* regular verbs use a form of the helping verb *have* with the **ed** form of the main verb, called the *past participle.*

EXAMPLES

PRESENT TENSE	SIMPLE PAST	PRESENT PERFECT
walk	walked	have walked
learn	learned	have learned
smile	smiled	have smiled

Irregular Verbs

7e **Irregular verbs usually show past tense by changing their spelling of the infinitive.**

Irregular verbs show past time in a different way. The verb *begin* is an example of an irregular verb. It shows the simple past in a special way. It does not add **ed** to the base form. Instead it changes its spelling to *began.*

EXAMPLES PRESENT TENSE
Today they *begin* their work.

SIMPLE PAST TENSE
Yesterday she *began* taking flute lessons.

Here are some irregular verbs in the present and simple past.

PRESENT	SIMPLE PAST
begin	began
do	did
drive	drove
ring	rang
take	took
throw	threw

EXERCISE 8 Number a sheet of paper from 1 to 10. Following are ten regular and irregular verbs. Some of the forms are missing. Next to each number write the form of the missing verb that belongs in each blank space. You may use a dictionary to help you.

EXAMPLE	PRESENT	SIMPLE PAST
	run	ran

	PRESENT	SIMPLE PAST
1.	do	_____
2.	speak	_____
3.	pull	_____
4.	_____	tried
5.	_____	rang
6.	poke	_____
7.	swim	_____
8.	drown	_____
9.	_____	threw
10.	crush	_____

Most irregular verbs show the *present perfect* by changing their spelling again. An example is the irregular verb *swim*. The past participle is *swum;*

with a form of the helping verb *have,* it forms the present perfect, *have swum.*

EXAMPLES

PRESENT   Terri *swims* a fast freestyle stroke.

SIMPLE PAST   Marie *swam* in the backstroke race.

PRESENT PERFECT   Nellie *has swum* in all her races.

Following are forms of irregular verbs that are used often.

PRESENT	SIMPLE PAST	PRESENT PERFECT
begin	began	have begun
break	broke	have broken
choose	chose	have chosen
do	did	have done
drive	drove	have driven
eat	ate	have eaten
fall	fell	have fallen
go	went	have gone
know	knew	have known
ride	rode	have ridden
see	saw	have seen
take	took	have taken
throw	threw	have thrown
wear	wore	have worn
write	wrote	have written

EXERCISE 9   Number a sheet of paper from 1 to 12. The following sentences have two forms of the verb. Next to each number write the correct form of the verb.

EXAMPLE   The announcer (begin/began) to talk
          to the crowd.

began

1. Last Saturday three of us (went/gone) to the
   fair.
2. Jill and Kerry (knew/known) what they wanted
   to wear.
3. They (wore/worn) old overalls.
4. I (wear/wore) slacks and my new red shirt.
5. I should have (chose/chosen) something else.
6. When Jill and Kerry (saw/seen) me, they
   laughed a little.
7. It (took/taken) us nearly an hour to get to the
   fair.
8. After we (get/got) there, we walked around and
   looked at the booths.
9. We (saw/seen) a lot of booths.
10. At one booth they (was/were) giving away tick-
    ets for a raffle.
11. But only those who (wore/worn) overalls could
    get a ticket.
12. I (know/knew) then why Jill and Kerry had
    laughed.

SPECIAL PRONOUN PROBLEMS

See Pronoun,
p. 270
See Noun,
p. 266 Pronouns take the place of nouns, noun word
groups, or other pronouns. Pronouns must agree in
number and sex with the nouns they replace.

Pronouns have several different forms. The
forms of personal pronouns, such as *I, me, he, him,
she, her, we,* and *us,* often cause problems.

7f   **The form of a pronoun depends upon how it is used in a sentence.**

(1)   **The pronoun subject of a sentence is in the subjective case.** See Case, p. 254

Study the following forms of the personal pronouns in the *subjective case.*

SUBJECTIVE CASE

Singular	Plural
I	we
you	you
he	
she	they
it	

EXAMPLES   Stella and *I* skated at the rink Saturday night.

She and *I* skated at the rink Saturday night.

We skated at the rink Saturday night.

(2)   **A personal pronoun used as an object is in the objective case.**

A personal pronoun that is the direct object of a verb is in the *objective case.* A personal pronoun that is the object of a preposition is also in the objective case.

Study the following forms of the personal pronouns in the objective case.

OBJECTIVE CASE

Singular	Plural
me	us
you	you
him	
her	them
it	

EXAMPLES   OBJECT OF THE VERB

Shari caught a big, ugly fish.
Shari caught *it*.
Then she caught more fish.
She cooked *them* for supper.

OBJECT OF A PREPOSITION

The mailman called to Mother and *me*.
The mailman called to *us*.
We went to the window and waved back at *him*.

EXERCISE 10   Number a sheet of paper from 1 to 5. Following are lists of personal pronouns. Some of the forms are missing in the subjective and objective cases. In rows next to each number write the forms that are missing.

	SUBJECTIVE CASE		OBJECTIVE CASE	
	Singular	Plural	Singular	Plural
1.	I	_____	me	_____
2.	_____	you	you	_____
3.	he	_____	_____	them
4.	_____	they	her	_____
5.	it	_____	it	_____

EXERCISE 11 Number a sheet of paper from 1 to 10. Next to each number write the correct form of the pronoun.

EXAMPLE Give the tickets to Barbara and (I, me).

me

1. Yetta and (she/her) want to learn to dance.
2. You and (I/me) might not have to.
3. Mark and (I/me) hate dancing.
4. I hope no one asks Mark or (I/me) to try.
5. Some others feel the way Mark and (I/me) feel.
6. They hate dancing the way Mark and (I/me) do.
7. They and (we/us) let Yetta and Joline try to dance together.
8. (She/Her) and Joline look funny out on the floor.
9. They can try without (we/us).
10. They and (we/us) will never go to dances together.

EXERCISE 12 Number a sheet of paper from 1 to 7. Next to each number write the correct form of the pronoun.

1. Gracie, why not come along with Carl and (I/me)?
2. He and (I/me) plan to ride on the bus.
3. It can take (we/us) as far as State Street.
4. Then (we/us) can walk to Lani's.
5. Lani should have some fresh cookies for (we/us) to eat.
6. I like them when (they/them) are hot.
7. (She/Her) and I eat too much.

PROBLEMS WITH ADJECTIVES AND ADVERBS

It is important to know when to use an adjective and when to use an adverb to modify other parts of a sentence.

See Linking
Verb, p. 265
See Subject,
p. 272

7g An adjective is used after a linking verb to modify the subject.

Do not use an adverb after a linking verb. Only an adjective can modify the noun or pronoun that is the subject of a linking verb.

EXAMPLES

RIGHT Mr. Atterburn seemed *sad*.
[The adjective *sad* modifies the subject by telling how Mr. Atterburn seemed.]

WRONG Mr. Atterburn seemed *sadly*.
[The adverb *sadly* cannot modify Mr. Atterburn because *seemed* is used as a linking verb.]

The word *good* is often used incorrectly. It is an adjective and should not be used as an adverb. The word *well* can be used as either an adverb or an adjective. (*Well* also may be used as a noun to describe a place where water is found.)

EXAMPLES

RIGHT This is a *good* pie. It tastes *good*.
WRONG I think you cook *good*.

RIGHT I think you cook *well*.
RIGHT The dog was *well* after the veterinarian left.

7h An adverb is used to modify an action verb.

Do not use an adjective to modify a verb.

EXAMPLES

RIGHT   Mrs. Diffwinkle flies *regularly* in her
         airplane.
         [*Regularly* is an adverb telling when
         the flying takes place.]

WRONG   Mrs. Diffwinkle flies *regular* in her
         airplane.
         [*Regular* is an adjective. It should not
         modify a verb.]

RIGHT   Mrs. Diffwinkle is a *regular* pilot.
         [*Regular* is an adjective modifying
         the noun *pilot.*]

EXERCISE 13   Each of the following sentences has
an error in the use of an adjective or an adverb.
Rewrite each sentence correctly.

EXAMPLE   Maisie and Candy cleaned up the
          hall good.

          *Maisie and Candy cleaned up
          the hall well.*

1. Meri Garfinkle thought the cake tasted sweetly.
2. She and Lois Tanner cook frequent.
3. Meri knows recipes good.
4. Lois is not badly at making bread.
5. They meet at Meri's house regular.
6. Meri's mother thinks both girls are well cooks.
7. Tom Tanner bakes good, too.

REVIEW EXERCISE A   Subject-Verb Agreement

Number your paper from 1 to 14. Rewrite each singular subject and verb to make it plural. Rewrite each plural subject and verb to make it singular.

EXAMPLE   The workmen cut

the workman cuts

1. the tall trees grow
2. the loggers save
3. the trees fall
4. the branch is trimmed
5. the logs go to the sawmill
6. the saw slices
7. the boards come out
8. the board is planed
9. the board dries
10. the carpenters hammer
11. the wall goes up
12. the walls are painted
13. the house is built
14. the people move in

REVIEW EXERCISE B   Correcting Subjects and Verbs

Some of the following sentences contain errors. Some have a singular subject but a plural verb. Others have a plural subject but a singular verb. Rewrite each sentence that has an error and make the necessary corrections.

EXAMPLE Many fierce storms begins near the North Pole.

Many fierce storms begin near the North Pole.

1. Cold air sweep down across Canada.
2. Areas of low pressure picks up moisture.
3. Heavy clouds form in the sky.
4. The cloud formations swirl in giant circles.
5. An area of low pressure moves clouds counter-clockwise.
6. Clouds with moisture drops snowflakes on the ground in winter.
7. A cloud going into southern states usually drop rain.
8. All of us is affected by storms.

REVIEW EXERCISE C Choosing the Correct Verb

Number a sheet of paper from 1 to 8. Next to each number write the correct form of the verb given in parentheses.

EXAMPLE José and Miguel (is/are) friends.

are

1. They and others on the street (plays/play) stickball.
2. Either José or some friends (brings/bring) the stick and a ball.
3. José and his sister Maria (hits/hit) the ball hard.
4. Miguel and two other boys (is/are) the fastest runners.

5. Pedestrians and traffic (disturbs/disturb) play.
6. On busy days Miguel or José (watches/watch) for cars.
7. A parked car or truck sometimes (blocks/block) the street.
8. If any rain or snow (is/are) on the street, it makes it harder to play.

REVIEW EXERCISE D   Regular and Irregular Verbs

Number a sheet of paper from 1 to 12. Following are regular and irregular verbs. The present or simple past tense forms is missing from each verb. Next to each number write the tense of the missing verb that belongs in each blank space.

EXAMPLE ring ___*rang*___

1. _____ chose
2. _____ knew
3. _____ rang
4. _____ saw
5. _____ ate
6. _____ did

7. break _____
8. throw _____
9. drown _____
10. drive _____
11. take _____
12. go _____

REVIEW EXERCISE E   Pronouns

Number a sheet of paper from 1 to 10. Next to each number write the correct form of the pronoun.

EXAMPLE Come with Jack and (I/me).

me

1. Is that dog barking at you or (I/me)?
2. You and (I/me) better walk quietly by.
3. Abby and (I/me) came last week.
4. I thought (he/him) and I had made friends.
5. He hardly growled at (we/us).
6. (We/Us) tried not to make him mad.
7. Others have told me he sometimes barks at (they/them).
8. We should feel lucky (he/him) is tied by a chain.
9. Did you say you think (he/him) has no chain now?
10. Does (he/him) know that?

REVIEW EXERCISE F   Adjectives and Adverbs

Each of the following sentences has an error in the use of an adjective or an adverb. Rewrite each sentence correctly.

EXAMPLE   Gerald Hornswoggle whispered careful in her ear.

Gerald Hornswoggle whispered carefully in her ear.

1. He told her she put on makeup good.
2. Her stockings looked sloppily, though.
3. Also, her shoes did not fit good.
4. She should brush her teeth more regular, he added.
5. And her messily hair might attract birds looking for a nest.
6. The dummy just kept looking steady out the store window while Gerald finished his work.

COMMON CONFUSIONS

This chapter will help you review some of the words that are most often confused or used incorrectly in the English language. You will learn why these mistakes may happen and what you can do to correct them.

See Article, p. 254

ALPHABETICAL LISTING

A/an: Use the article *an* before words that start with the sounds these letters stand for: **a, e, i, o,** and **u.**

EXAMPLES   *an* apple, ape, axe, awful thing
an egg, elephant, ear, extra piece
an igloo, idiot, ill person
an ox, orange, only child, honest person
an uncle, umpire, unhappy person

Use the article *a* before words beginning with the sounds of *all* other letters.

EXAMPLES   *a* bat, case, dog, fish, goat, house
a jack, king, liar, man, nut, pet
a queen, rat, ship, truck, unicorn
a very nice person, whale
a yellow submarine, zebra

Notice that no **x** word is given. Almost all words that begin with **x** are said with **z** sounds; for example, *xylophone. X-ray* begins with an **e** sound, like that in *extra.*

Accept/except: *Accept* means "to agree to receive something." It is a verb.

EXAMPLES   It is hard to *accept* criticism.
It is easy to *accept* money.

Except means "leaving out" or "but." It is a preposition.

EXAMPLES   I'll eat everything *except* that raw green pepper.
Everyone came *except* Barb.

EXERCISE 1   Write the following sentences on a sheet of paper. Then fill in each blank with *accept* or *except.*

1. I will not _____ a dare.
2. I like all sports _____ football.
3. Don't _____ his excuse for hitting that little child.
4. Everyone _____ Toni has been to my house.

Advice/advise: *Advice* is a noun that means "an opinion, information, or suggestion that someone gives."

EXAMPLES   Her *advice* was to stay out of fights.
            That sounds like good *advice* to me.

Advise is a verb that means "to give an opinion, information, or suggestion."

EXAMPLES   I *advise* you not to get into a fight.
            She *advises* everyone to go.

EXERCISE 2   Write the following sentences on a sheet of paper. Then fill in each blank with *advice* or *advise*.

1. Her best friend always gives her good _____ .
2. That friend would always _____ her not to lie.
3. I took her _____ .
4. I _____ you to quit shoving.

Am not, are not, is not/ain't: *Ain't* is a word that some people may use in speaking to stand for *am not, are not,* or *is not. Ain't* has a long history of use. However, it is generally accepted only for very informal usuage.

WRITE   I *am not* chewing loudly.
         not
         I *ain't* chewing loudly.

WRITE   He *isn't* doing anything.
         not
         He *ain't* doing anything.

WRITE   We *aren't* going.
         not
         We *ain't* going.

When you speak or write, use *am not, aren't,* or *isn't* instead of *ain't.*

EXERCISE 3 Write the following sentences on a sheet of paper. Use *am not, are not,* or *is not* in place of *ain't.*

1. I ain't going to do it.
2. That letter ain't at my house.
3. The buses ain't here yet.
4. I ain't asking again.

All right/alright: *All right* is correctly written as two words. *Alright* is not a word in English.

Almost/most: *Almost* means "very nearly."

EXAMPLES   She is *almost* fifteen.
            Almost everybody in my class is
            older.

Most can mean "more than anything else."

EXAMPLES   It was the *most* horrible movie I
            ever saw.
            She was the *most* excited person
            I've ever seen.

Most can also mean "the greatest amount."

EXAMPLES   She had *most* of the junk hidden
            somewhere.
            We have come *most* of the way.

Sometimes *most* can mean "almost all."

EXAMPLES   I like *most* vegetables.
            I am here *most* of the time.

Most should not be used as a short form of *almost*.

WRITE　She is *almost* done.

　　　　not

　　　　She is *most* done.

WRITE　She ate *most* of the cookies.

　　　　not

　　　　She ate *most* all the cookies.

EXERCISE 4　Write the following sentences on a sheet of paper. Replace *most* with *almost* wherever it is needed. Some sentences do not need correcting.

1. Most everything was done for them.
2. Most of them came late.
3. She likes most of those.
4. She likes most all of those.

Already/all ready: *Already* means "by this time" or "before now."

EXAMPLES　I *already* know how to read.

　　　　　　I have learned that *already*.

The words *all* and *ready* are two different words which mean "all of something is ready."

EXAMPLES　They are *all ready* to learn how to drive.

　　　　　　Is everyone *all ready* to go?

Do not confuse the one word *already* with the two words *all* and *ready*.

WRITE　Most of us are *all ready* to leave.

　　　　not

　　　　Most of us are *already* to leave.

WRITE   Are we *all ready*?
not
Are we *already*?

EXERCISE 5   Write the following sentences on a sheet of paper. Fill in each blank with *already* or *all ready*.

1. They must be there _____ .
2. The students are _____ to go.
3. Are we _____ there?
4. Are they _____ now?
5. I think I've _____ done it.
6. We are _____ to leave.

Can/may: *Can* means "to know how to do something" or "to be able to do something."

EXAMPLES   I *can* do algebra problems better than geometry problems.
I *can* dance if I want to.

May means "something is possible or likely" or "someone is to be allowed to do something."

EXAMPLES   She says she *may* come if she has time.
May I go?

Use *may* when you mean "to ask or give permission."

WRITE   *May* I have it?
not
Can I have it?
WRITE   You *may* go now.
not
You *can* go now.

EXERCISE 6   Write the following sentences on a sheet of paper. Put *may* or *can* in each blank.

1. You know you _____ do it, if you try.
2. No, you _____ not go now!
3. _____ you work those problems?
4. She _____ have the answer.
5. _____ we try, too?

Can hardly/can't hardly: *Hardly* means "barely." *Can hardly* means "can barely."

> EXAMPLES   He *can hardly* do it.
> (It's hard. He can barely do it.)
>
> I *can hardly* reach it.
> (I can just barely reach it.)

Always write *can hardly*, never write *can't hardly*.

> WRITE   I *can hardly* see.
> not
> I *can't hardly* see.
> WRITE   I *can hardly* understand.
> not
> I *can't hardly* understand.

Cannot/can not: Both ways of writing the word are all right. They both mean "not able to." *Can not* gives more emphasis to a statement.

> EXAMPLE   She *cannot* be here. She *can not* be here.

Could have/could of: People write *could of* by mistake. When you say *could have* quickly, it usually sounds like "could've." "Could've" sounds like "could of," and so you may write it down wrong.

WRITE   I *could have* done it.
         not
         I *could of* done it.

WRITE   She *could have* been a great diver.
         not
         She *could of* been a great diver.

Good/well: *Good* means "better than the usual or the average."

EXAMPLES   This is really *good* ice cream.
            He did a *good* job.

Well means "in a way that is good or pleasing."

EXAMPLES   She did it *well*.
            He really draws people *well*.

Good is an adjective, a word that describes a noun.

EXAMPLES   She's a *good* friend.
            That's a *good* place.

Well is usually an adverb, a word that describes a verb.

EXAMPLES   She runs *well*.
            That works *well*.

WRITE   She sings *well*.
         not
         She sings *good*.

WRITE   He did the job *well*.
         not
         He did the job *good*.

EXERCISE 7   Write the following sentences on a sheet of paper. Fill in each blank with *good* or *well*.

1. He did that _____ .
2. What a _____ job she did.
3. Joan is running _____ now.
4. That was very _____ done.

I/me: *I* means "the person speaking or writing."

EXAMPLES *I* am very thirsty.
          I like hot dogs.

Me means "the person who receives the action" or "the person something is done to."

EXAMPLES She likes *me*.
          The donkey bit *me*.

WRITE Andy and *I* went downtown.
       not
       Andy and *me* went downtown.

WRITE Beth and *I* will go.
       not
       Beth and *me* will go.

EXERCISE 8   Write the following sentences on a sheet of paper. Fill in each blank with *I* or *me*.

1. I saw the dog. The dog saw _____ .
2. She doesn't like me. _____ don't like her.
3. I pushed Harry. Harry pushed _____ .
4. She and I took Paul and John to the movies. Then Paul and John took her and _____ to the hamburger stand.
5. They like her and me. She and _____ like them, too.

Its/it's: *Its* is a possessive word. The letter **s** on the end either means "ownership, owning something," or it means that "the thing which follows is a part of it."

EXAMPLES I like the sweater because of *its* color. (*Color* is a part of it.)
Do you like *its* looks? (*Looks* is a part of it.)

It's means the same thing as *it is*. The apostrophe (') stands for the missing letter **i** in the word *is*.

EXAMPLES *It's* not fun to play with someone who cheats.
It's ready now.

EXERCISE 9 Copy the following sentences on a sheet of paper. Correct any mistakes in the use of *its* and *it's*.

1. I like it's color.
2. I think its mine.
3. Get out of its way.
4. Its a pain in the neck.
5. Its theirs.
6. What is its meaning?

Learn/teach: *Learn* and *teach* have different meanings. Someone *teaches* something *to* someone. Someone *learns* something *from* someone.
    Remember: A learner or student *learns from* a teacher. A teacher *teaches* something *to* a learner.

Lie/lay: *Lie* has two meanings. One is "to tell an untruth."

EXAMPLE Do not *lie* to me about the money.

The other meaning for *lie* is "to lie down."

EXAMPLE *Lie* on the couch to rest.

The past tense of the *lie* meaning "an untruth" is regular.

EXAMPLE He *lied* about the money.

The past tense of the *lie* meaning "to lie down" is irregular.

EXAMPLE She *lay* on the couch to rest. (The action of lying is in the past.)

Lay is the verb to use when you put something down.

EXAMPLE I will *lay* the gun on the desk.

EXERCISE 10   Write the following sentences on a piece of paper. Fill in each blank with the correct form of *lie* or *lay*.

1. He _____ on his back and looked at the sky.
2. The old Bible _____ on the bookshelf.
3. If you _____ again, how can I ever believe you?
4. _____ down your weapons and surrender.
5. You tricked me because you _____ to me.

OK, O.K., Okay/all right: All of the three spellings of *okay* are common. In writing, it is usually better to use *all right* instead of *okay*.

Set/sit: These two words are often confused. *Set* is the word to use when you put something in a certain way or place:

EXAMPLES He *set* the knife down.
          She *set* the table.

Sit is the word to use when telling about an action of a person or an animal.

EXAMPLES Teachers always make students *sit* down.
The lions *sit* quietly.

WRITE I will *set* it down.
not
I will *sit* it down.

WRITE Please *sit* down.
not
Please *set* down.

EXERCISE 11 Write these sentences on a sheet of paper. Fill in the blanks with *set* or *sit*.

1. Please _____ by me.
2. She _____ the platter on the table.
3. He will _____ by the window.
4. Jack _____ the table.

Should have/should of: People write *should of* by mistake. When they say "should have" quickly, it usually sounds like "should've." "Should've" sounds like "should of," and so people may write it down wrong.

WRITE I *should have* done it.
not
I *should of* done it.

WRITE She *should have* been a great player.
not
She *should of* been a great player.

Those/them (there): *Them* and *them there* should not be written instead of *those*.

WRITE   *Those* books . . . *Those* people . . .
not
Them books . . . *Them there* people . . .

EXERCISE 12   Write the following sentences on a sheet of paper. Use *those* instead of *them* and *them there*.

1. Some of them things are really nice.
2. I got mad at them people.
3. Them there are the ones.
4. Some of them there words are hard to say.

Their/there/they're: These three words are often said the same way. They are *homonyms*. *Their* is a word that shows ownership. It is the possessive form of the pronoun *they*.

EXAMPLES   Sarah is *their* chimpanzee.
We are going to *their* house.

There tells where something happens. It is an adverb.

EXAMPLES   I saw them *there*.
I met her *there*.

They're means *they* plus *are*.

EXAMPLES   *They're* here now.
They're the ones I mean.

Because these three words sound alike, they may cause spelling errors.

EXERCISE 13   Write the following sentences on a sheet of paper. Correct every spelling error in the use of *their, there,* or *they're*.

1. That's they're house over their.
2. There dog bit the mail carrier.
3. Let's go their.
4. They're they are.
5. I like they're looks.
6. There friends think there moving.
7. Their are many ways there wrong.

These, this, that/these here, this here, that there: *These* and *this* mean something close; they do not need the extra word *here* to make their meaning clear. *That* means something farther away; it does not need the extra word *there* to make its meaning clear. *Them there* is considered non-standard English.

WRITE   *These* things are hard.
　　　　 not
　　　　 These here things are hard.

WRITE   *That* book is closed.
　　　　 not
　　　　 That there book is closed.

WRITE   *Those* cars are clean.
　　　　 not
　　　　 Them there cars are clean.

EXERCISE 14 Write the following sentences on a sheet of paper. Correct them by taking out the words *here* and *there* when they are not needed.

1. Then they met this here strange-looking man.
2. That there frog sure can jump.
3. That there alligator just swallowed Susie.
4. This here is a pretty one.

To/too/two: These three words are pronounced the same. They are *homonyms*. The word *to* usually introduces another word or group of words.

EXAMPLES   *to* him, *to* the lake, *to* be pleased

Too means "also."

EXAMPLES   I want some, *too.* I can do it, *too.*

Two is a number meaning "one more than one."

EXAMPLES   He had *two* pet snails. I had *two,* too.

Because all three words are said alike, they may cause spelling problems.

EXERCISE 15   Write the following sentences on a sheet of paper. Correct every spelling error in the use of *to, too,* or *two.*

1. To snails are two many.
2. If you knew snails, you'd think so, to.
3. She took hers too the zoo.
4. I took my to too the zoo, two.

Who/whom: *Who* and *whom* are different forms of the same word. In most cases, *who* is used.

EXAMPLES   *Who* tried the hardest?
           Who wants some gum?

Who should not be used after a word like *to, from,* or *for.*

WRITE   to *whom,* for *whom,* from *whom*
        not
        to *who,* for *who,* from *who*

Whose/who's: These two words are pronounced alike. They are *homonyms. Whose* is a form of *who* that shows ownership or possession.

EXAMPLES *Whose* house did you go to? (Who owns the house?)
I know *whose* mitt that is. (I know who the mitt belongs to.)

Who's is a form of *who* and *is*. The apostrophe (') takes the place of the letter **i** in the word *is* or the letters **ha** in the word *has*.

EXAMPLES She's always the one *who's* right.
Who's got the nerve to try it?

Remember: Use *who's* only when you mean *who is* or *who has.*

EXERCISE 16 Write each of the following sentences that has a *whose/who's* error in it on a sheet of paper. Correct the error.

1. Whose going to tell her she won all that money?
2. Whose motorcycle is that?
3. I know who's money that is.
4. Whose allowed to watch the late horror movies?
5. Whose the boy whose hanging around there?

Your/you're: These two words are pronounced alike. They are *homonyms. Your* is the possessive form of *you*. It shows ownership.

EXAMPLES It is *your* problem now.
Did you get *your* letter from the table?

You're stands for *you* and *are.*

EXAMPLES   *You're* my best friend.

Are you sure *you're* right?

EXERCISE 17   Write each of the following sentences on a piece of paper. Choose the correct homonym.

1. (You're/Your) mother called today.
2. She said that (you're/your) to go to your grandmother's house.
3. (You're/Your) willing to do (you're/your) best for her, aren't you?
4. She's often said (you're/your) her favorite.
5. (You're/Your) great aunt has said that (you're/your) her favorite, too.

REVIEW EXERCISE A

Number your paper from 1 to 10. Next to each number write the correct form from those in parentheses.

EXAMPLE   It was (a/an) exciting party, (accept/except) for the ending.

an, except

1. Would you (advice/advise) Velma to (accept/except) the invitation?
2. (Isn't/Ain't) it (all right/alright) to go?
3. She is (almost/most) too late to (accept/except).
4. It was (almost/most) (a/an) unexpected party.
5. She had (all ready/already) planned to be (all ready/already) when the time came.
6. She (all ready/already) knew she would be among several friends.

7. The time between getting ready and going seemed (almost/most) forever.
8. She (can hardly/can't hardly) wait.
9. She (could of/could have) been (all ready/already) much earlier.
10. The early part was the (almost/most) interesting, but the ending (could have/could of) been more fun.

REVIEW EXERCISE B

For each of the following sentences, follow the same instructions as given for Review Exercise A.

1. The (good/well) scores go to those who play (good/well).
2. If Wally and (I/me) practice, he and (I/me) can both win.
3. (It's/Its) going to be a close match for him and (I/me).
4. As the match neared (it's/its) end, my feet felt like lead.
5. Wally had me (set/sit) down so he could (learn/teach) me to correct a mistake.
6. He told me I (should have/should of) made (them/those) easy shots.
7. "(They're/There) easy," he said, "when the opponents feed (there/their) shots to you."
8. I said I would (try and/try to) make (these here/these) shots in the future.
9. "(Who's/Whose) ball was that?" he shouted, when the ball whistled by (to/too) fast for either of us.
10. "It was (your/you're) ball," I answered, "because it came (to/too) you."

UNIT FOUR

MECHANICS

Capitalization
Punctuation

CAPITALIZATION

The alphabet, as you know, has twenty-six letters. Every letter has two forms. One form is a *capital* letter. The other form is a small letter. To write correctly you need to know when to use one form or the other. This chapter will help you understand when to use capital letters. It will also help you understand why capital letters are useful.

CAPITAL LETTERS

9a Capitalize the first word in a sentence.

Make sure every sentence you write begins with a capital letter. The first word in a quotation should also begin with a capital letter.

EXAMPLES Four eggs broke. Out came four tiny alligators.

Bessie screamed, "We can't have scrambled eggs for breakfast!"

9b Capitalize the pronoun *I*.

See Pronoun,
p. 270

Do not capitalize any other pronoun unless it begins a sentence.

EXAMPLES This week **I** hope to see my uncle.
He promised me a job this summer.

9c Capitalize proper nouns.

See Noun,
p. 266

Proper nouns are names of particular people, places, or things. They should be capitalized. John Wayne and Francie Larrieu, for example, are special people. Their names are capitalized. The Snake River and Madison Square Garden are special places.

EXAMPLES **John Wayne, Francie Larrieu** (but not *man* or *woman*)
the **Snake River** (but not *river*)
Ford Granada (but not *car*)

(1) Capitalize the names of particular people and animals.

EXAMPLES Come in, **Mrs. Masser**. Watch out for our mean cat, **Whiskers**. He bit **Freddie Teiz** on the ear, and **Dr. Soadumup** had to bandage it.

(2) Capitalize the names of particular places.

EXAMPLES

Cities, Towns	San Diego, Detroit, Gary
States, Counties	Illinois, Cook County
Nations	United States, Saudi Arabia
Continents	Europe, Africa
Roadways	Broadway, Elm Avenue, Northway Turnpike
Bodies of Water	Lake Placid, the Red Sea
Islands, Points of Land	Manhattan Island, Hawaii Cape Cod, Mount McKinley
Special Regions	the Southwest, Appalachia, the Middle East
Parks	Yellowstone, Disneyland

Do not capitalize directions.

EXAMPLES "Go west, young man," said
Greeley.
"Go down, Moses," is part of an
old song.

EXERCISE 1 Number a sheet of paper from 1 to
10. After each number write the correct form of the
proper nouns or the pronoun *I* in each sentence.

EXAMPLE We saw george washington standing
by the river.

George Washington

1. It was almost an accident that christopher columbus came to america.
2. The explorer thought that he had found india.
3. He didn't know that america and the pacific ocean were in his way.
4. Later, a man named amerigo vespucci claimed to have explored the coast.
5. Explorers from england, spain, france, and italy all crossed the atlantic ocean to see what was going on.
6. In those days, there were no big cities like new york, chicago, or boston.
7. No one had even thought of miami or atlanta.
8. Disneyland, mickey and minnie mouse, and donald duck were all hundreds of years in the future.
9. Instead, the people who already lived in what would become the united states had learned skills to help them survive.
10. I wonder what columbus would think of america now.

EXERCISE 2 Number a sheet of paper from 1 to 10. The proper nouns and the pronoun I in the following sentences have no capital letters. After each number write the correct form of the proper nouns or pronouns in each sentence.

EXAMPLE   Datsuns, toyotas, and other small cars are very popular in saudi arabia.

Toyotas, Saudi Arabia.

1. Buffalo bill spent much of his life in texas and wyoming.

2. Next week, i hope to visit laramie, wyoming.
3. The town of cheyenne is also supposed to be very interesting.
4. Frankly, i don't see how any place can be very interesting once the buffalo are gone.
5. At one time, great herds of buffalo roamed the west and southwest.
6. The Native americans used parts of the buffalo for almost everything.
7. The buffalo was as useful to the Native americans as the seal is useful to the eskimo today.
8. In the san diego zoo, i saw a couple of buffalo.
9. The yaks today in tibet are said to be like the buffalo of old in america.
10. Someday, i would like to see the wildlife in parts of asia.

(3) Capitalize the names of races, religions, and nationalities.

EXAMPLES

Races	Caucasian, Negro, (*Black* is also used), Native American
Religions	Baptist, Jewish, Buddhist
Nationalities	Irish, Iranian, Nigerian

(4) Capitalize the important words in the names of organizations, institutions, companies and their products, and government bodies.

When only initials are written, capitalize them. Usually periods are omitted from initials.

EXAMPLES

Organizations	Amateur Athletic Union (**AAU**) North Atlantic Treaty Organization (**NATO**)
Institutions	Bright Junior High, University of Southern California (**USC**)
Companies	General Motors (**GM**), Volkswagen (**VW**), Speedee skateboard, Avon curlers [Notice that only the brand name is capitalized, not the following common noun.]
Government Bodies	Congress, the Supreme Court

(5) **Capitalize school subjects when they are used as names of courses.**

EXAMPLES I took Art History to learn more about art.
In General Math we study practical mathematics.
Our teacher said we would have some biographies to read during Social Studies class.

EXERCISE 3 Number a sheet of paper from 1 to 10. Some of the following sentences are correct. Some need capital letters. For each correct sentence, write *C* after the number. For the others, write the correct form of each word needing a capital letter.

EXAMPLE   lowell junior high has a woman from nigeria teaching a course called african history.

Lowell Junior High, Nigeria, African History.

1. A herd of elephants from india invaded flatt junior high school last week.
2. The National Wildlife Federation sent a photographer.
3. The national guard sent general zabriski and some soldiers to protect the cafeteria.
4. An elephant trainer from the university of georgia was asked for advice.
5. The elephants came to some of the classes, including General Math and Social Science.
6. They seemed most interested in Greek and Roman history.
7. "Hannibal, an ambitious general, used elephants to cross the alps," our teacher said.
8. The ford foundation gave the school money to study elephants in grades seven and eight.
9. The amateur athletic union and the supreme court objected to the use of elephants on the flatt football team.
10. Finally, after studying hard, two elephants went on to Flatt High School.

(6) Capitalize titles of people, the first word and all important words in the titles of books, magazines, newspapers, movies, television shows, and other works people produce.

EXAMPLES

People	General Custer, Senator Smith, Uncle Ben (but not *his uncle*), Officer Wheeler (but not any officer)
Books, Stories, Poems	the Bible, *Treasure Island*, "Evangeline"
Magazines	*Teentime, Newsweek*
Newspapers	the *Denver Post*, the *National Observer*
Movies	*King Kong, Son of the Sheik*
TV shows	"Creature Features," "Wide World of Sports"
Works in Music, Art, Architecture	"Moonlight Sonata," the *Mona Lisa*, the Taj Mahal

(7) Capitalize the name of God and other beings worshipped by people.

EXAMPLES God, Jehovah, the Almighty, Jupiter, Buddha

(8) Capitalize the name of historical events, periods, or other special events.

EXAMPLES the Great Depression, the American Revolution, Mother's Day, the Fourth of July

EXERCISE 4   Copy the following sentences on your paper. Put capitals where they belong.

> EXAMPLE   Julian invited Marie to go to the movies to see *the return of wonder woman.*
>
> *Julian invited Marie to go to the movies to see The Return of Wonder Woman.*

1. King kong spent the fourth of july visiting the empire state building.
2. The *washington post* reported his visit.
3. The evening news on nbc ran parts of an old king kong movie.
4. The giant gorilla told a reporter from *newsweek* that he was just another tourist.
5. "The days of beating my chest like tarzan are over," king kong added.

EXERCISE 5   Number a sheet of paper from 1 to 5. After each number write *a* or *b* to show which sentence is correct.

> EXAMPLE   a. I visited Aunt Juanita on the Fourth of July.
>   b. I visited aunt juanita on the fourth of july.
>
> *a*

1. a.   General Easter called the Chicago *Tribune.*
   b.   General easter called the chicago *tribune.*
2. a.   Last night we saw the old movie *the gold rush* with charlie chaplin.
   b.   Last night we saw the old movie *The Gold Rush* with Charlie Chaplin.

3. a. Our teacher, mr. roberts, likes to watch *happy days* on television.
   b. Our teacher, Mr. Roberts, likes to watch "Happy Days" on television.
4. a. *The Sword in the Stone* is a book about King Arthur and the Middle Ages.
   b. The *sword in the stone* is a book about king arthur and the middle ages.
5. a. During the golden age of greece, jupiter was considered the most powerful god on mount olympus.
   b. During the Golden Age of Greece, Jupiter was considered the most powerful god on Mount Olympus.

9d Capitalize proper adjectives.

A proper adjective begins with a capital letter. It is a word made from a proper noun.

EXAMPLES   The display of Chinese art was in the museum.
The Arabian custom required the host to kill a sheep for his guests.

EXERCISE 6   Six of the following words are proper adjectives. They should have capitals. On your paper write the six proper adjectives from the list. Capitalize them.

EXAMPLE   english

English

english, ten, canadian, japanese, pottery, georgian, similar, mexican, oceanic, african

REVIEW EXERCISE A   Capitalization

Number a sheet of paper from 1 to 10. Some capital letters have been omitted from words in the following sentences. After each number write the word or words needing capital letters. Capitalize them correctly.

1. Last week, i saw my uncle in Arizona. he lives in a cave near phoenix.
2. A cat named napoleon lives there also.
3. They have lived in chicago, new york, paris, and a small town called catsville.
4. My uncle's name is bob katz.
5. "My pet is a persian cat," uncle bob told me.
6. Looking up from *time* magazine, the cat meowed with a slight iranian accent.
7. Together, the three of us went to see the london bridge at lake havasu.
8. Arizona was so sunny we went everywhere in my uncle's volkswagen with the sunroof open.
9. "This car from germany is very comfortable," my uncle said.
10. "Yes," napoleon agreed. "It's purr-fect."

REVIEW EXERCISE B   More Capitalization

Copy the following sentences. Put in capital letters where they are needed.

1. Roy rogers pulled up his horse trigger, not the trigger of his gun.
2. In the bible, god told noah to build an ark to save the animals.

3. In *time,* i read about a marsupial from madagascar.

4. I took general science to study plants and animals.

5. Some cars, such as the cougar, pinto, and mustang, are named after animals.

6. The movie, *born free,* was about a lion named elsa.

7. The national wildlife association and the audubon society try to protect animals.

8. In india, members of the hindu religion consider the cows to be sacred animals.

9. Years ago in the west and southwest, cowboys thought their horses were very important.

10. No one ever asked the horses in texas what they thought of the cowboys.

10

PUNCTUATION

End Punctuation, Commas

Read these two sentences aloud.

I heard what Mac said.   He is wrong.

Notice how different punctuation shows other ways of saying these two sentences.

I heard what Mac said.   He is wrong!
I heard what Mac said.   He is wrong?
I heard what Mac said.   "He is wrong."

The words in all four sets of sentences remain the same. The meanings change, however. Punctuation marks help to show in writing what the tones and loudness of the voice show in speaking.

END PUNCTUATION

Certain kinds of punctuation are used to mark the endings of sentences. These kinds are the period, the question mark, and the exclamation mark. They help to show how these sentences should be read.

The Period

10a A period is used to mark the end of a statement or a request.

EXAMPLES He can see in the dark.
Please close the drapes.

10b A period is used after some abbreviations.

EXAMPLES Oak Ave.   A.M.
Nov.   B.C.

10c A period is usually used after an initial.

EXAMPLES May T. Sumter
This dime was coined in the U.S. Mint.

Some sets of initials that are often used omit periods.

EXAMPLES USA   JFK
USSR   NASA

EXERCISE 1 On a separate sheet of paper write the following sentences. Put in periods where they are missing and circle them.

EXAMPLE   P T Barnum was a great showman.

P₀ T₀ Barnum was a great showman.

1. Phineas T Barnum was born in Bethel, Conn, on July 5, 1810
2. He made a fortune with C S Stratton, a midget he renamed Gen Tom Thumb
3. Barnum brought a huge elephant named Jumbo to the U S in 1882
4. Later he joined with J A Bailey to form a large circus
5. Today it is called the Ringling Bros and Barnum & Bailey Circus

The Question Mark

10d A question mark is used to mark the end of a sentence that asks a question.

EXAMPLES   Do you like spiders?
How fast can you run?

EXERCISE 2 Number a sheet of paper from 1 to 6. Put a period after the number of each statement or request. Put a question mark after the number of each question.

1. Please open the door
2. Where did you put the box
3. We had a dozen apples all together
4. Can she find any
5. This is a rotten one
6. Do some go bad in hot weather

The Exclamation Mark

10e **An exclamation mark is used at the end of a strong statement.**

The statement may be in the form of a complete sentence, a phrase, or a word.

EXAMPLES You have no right to do that!
A neat trick!
Danger!
Help!

EXERCISE 3 Number a sheet of paper from 1 to 6. Put a period after the number of each statement or request. Put a question mark after the number of each question. Put an exclamation mark after the number of each exclamation.

1. What nonsense that is
2. Can you do better
3. All attempts may fail
4. Look out
5. Now and then we nap
6. How long is the trip

INSIDE PUNCTUATION

Punctuation that comes inside a sentence usually separates parts of the sentence. The comma is the punctuation mark most often used inside the sentence. Other marks are used in some cases. This section shows you the common uses of the comma.

The Comma

10f **A comma is used between items in a series.**

Three or more items together make a series. Commas set them apart from each other.

EXAMPLES   Betty Rantyer raised turkeys, hogs, and sheep.
[words in a series]

Luann beat Derek 6-3, 6-2, 6-4.
[numerals in a series]

You will find flowers in the mountains, in the valleys, and on the plains.
[phrases in a series]

Some people prefer to omit the comma before the conjunction connecting the last two items in a series. Follow your teacher's instructions in this.

EXERCISE 4   Copy the following ten sentences on a sheet of paper. Put in commas where they are missing.

1. National parks in the United States are located in the East the South the Midwest and the West.
2. The national parks cover more than fourteen million acres of mountains plains canyons deserts and islands.
3. Each year millions of people visit the parks to see the sights to hike the trails and to camp outdoors.
4. The nation's three largest parks are Yellowstone Mt. McKinley and the Everglades.

5. In Yellowstone one can visit the world's largest area of geysers giant waterfalls canyons and wild life regions.

6. The Grand Canyon offers colored rock walls steep trails and a rushing river in a mile-deep canyon.

7. California is proud of its five parks: Kings Canyon Park Lassen Volcanic Park Sequoia Park Redwood Park and Yosemite Park.

8. The parks of Bryce Canyon Canyonlands and Zion are in Utah.

9. Arizona Colorado Hawaii Montana Texas and Washington each have two national parks.

10. People travel to the parks on foot by cycle in cars or by bus.

10g Commas are used to set off items that interrupt a sentence.

Interrupters may be single words or phrases.

EXAMPLES The winner of the contest, *Wilma*, was made mayor for a day.
My brother, *the leader of the group*, wants to leave tomorrow.

(1) Commas set off appositives.

An *appositive* is a word or phrase that repeats the meaning of the word or phrase it follows. Because it interrupts the flow of the sentence, it is set off with commas.

EXAMPLES Lynn, *one of our best swimmers*, broke her leg on Saturday.
We painted her cast blue and gold, *our school colors*.

EXERCISE 5   Number a sheet of paper from 1 to 10. The following sentences need commas to set off interrupting words or phrases. After each number, write the interrupting words or phrases. Put commas where they belong.

> EXAMPLE   I once had a stuffed clown a kind of doll sitting in a corner of my bedroom.

, a kind of doll,

1. Dolls those playthings of childhood have a long history.
2. Millions of children mostly girls enjoy playing with dolls.
3. Boys also enjoy the imaginary world one of make-believe that goes with dolls.
4. Some of the boys' toys soldiers or other figures are like dolls.
5. Countless children perhaps millions have enjoyed imagining their dolls were alive.
6. Georgette Baker a girl in our neighborhood collected all kinds of dolls for five years.
7. One of her dolls a Kachina doll came from the Hopi Indians a tribe in the Southwest.
8. Georgette also had a Kalifa a special doll from Africa.
9. In ancient Rome a country on the Mediterranean Sea young girls owned dolls made of wood or clay.
10. Just before getting married, a girl would leave her dolls on the altar of Diana a goddess of young women.

(2) Commas set off words like *yes, no,* and *well* when they are added as interrupters in a sentence.

EXAMPLES *No*, that lemon is too sour.
Well, should I put sugar on it?

(3) Commas set off transitional terms.

Transitional terms show an idea or a thought that continues from one sentence to another. They help the reader follow the flow of thought from sentence to sentence. Transitional terms are sometimes called parenthetical expressions. They should be set apart from the main thought of a sentence by a comma.

EXAMPLES *To be truthful*, the ball was out of bounds. *In fact*, it was pretty far out. *Of course*, you can have the point. It seems unfair to me, *however*.

EXERCISE 6 Copy the following sentences. Put in commas where they are missing.

1. We wish you well of course.
2. However you must watch out for gremlins.
3. Gremlins as you know creep into many corners.
4. Yes but how can one protect against them?
5. You are in danger if in fact a gremlin is around.
6. Well to be honest we invite them in by our carelessness.

(4) Commas set off terms of direct address.

When a sentence addresses someone directly, the name of the person should be set off with commas. It interrupts the flow of the sentence.

EXAMPLES   Frankie, stop that noise!
But that noise is necessary, Mrs. Bumbleberry.
Not inside, you idiot, or you will disturb the bees.

EXERCISE 7 Copy the following five sentences onto a sheet of paper. Insert commas where they are needed.

1. Stop the elevator when it gets to our floor Mike.
2. Wait a minute Archie or Mike will be late.
3. You must be joking General about our troops being tardy
4. No one I tell you can be more serious.
5. I can take Mike and Archie down again sir.

10h A comma is used between adjectives not joined by the conjunction *and*.

EXAMPLES   Nadia soared in a tumbling, twisting leap.
Nellie fell in an awkward, sprawling heap.

Do not, however, put a comma between adjectives if the second adjective is closely connected to the noun.

EXAMPLES The tan sheep dog ran at the
coyote.
[The adjective *sheep* is closely
connected to the noun *dog*.]

The old rag doll lay on the bed.
[The adjective *rag* is closely
connected to the noun *doll*.]

EXERCISE 8 Number a sheet of paper from 1 to 5.
After each number write the adjectives that need a
comma to separate them. Put in the missing commas. One sentence needs no comma.

EXAMPLE The rearing plunging horse drew
attention.

rearing, plunging

1. Learning gymnastics takes serious hard training.
2. Good gymnasts succeed only because of thorough
regular practice.
3. The balance beam is a long narrow piece of
wood.
4. It requires strength and balance to perform
difficult gymnastic tricks.
5. The slow awkward person must work hard to become a graceful winning performer.

10i **A comma is used before a conjunction
joining independent statements in a
compound sentence.**

See Conjunc-
tion, p. 257

EXAMPLES We raced up the hill to the
tower, but Redbeard and his men
had already gone.
Pirates will stop at nothing, and
I fear these will go farther than
most.

A short compound sentence usually needs no comma.

EXAMPLE She turned and he fled.

EXERCISE 9 Number a sheet of paper from 1 to 5. Each following sentence is a compound sentence with two independent statements. Beside each number write the last word of the first independent statement. Then write the conjunction that connects it to the second independent statement. Finally, put a comma between the statements if one belongs there.

EXAMPLE We could see the remains of their
campfire but the men had
completely disappeared.

campfire, but

1. The hilltop gave us a sweeping view of the harbor and the town but we could see no sign of life.
2. It seems that the pirates had melted away but we knew they could not escape by sea.
3. Our ships had been patrolling the seacoast since we landed and no boats had gone out or come in.
4. We were puzzled but we did not relax.
5. We knew the pirates had to come out in a day or two or they would die of starvation and thirst.

10j Commas are used in certain standard forms.

(1) A comma is used before quotation marks.

EXAMPLE   Drexel called to Ginger, "Come
home now," in a voice so loud the
neighbors heard him.

(2) A comma is used to set off names of cities or towns from states and countries.

EXAMPLE   They mean Portsmouth, New
Hampshire, and not Portsmouth,
England.

(3) Commas separate items in dates.

EXAMPLES   New Orleans, Louisiana, became
an American city on December 20,
1803.
On July 8, 1947, the town dump
caught fire.

EXERCISE 10   Copy the following five sentences.
Put in commas where they are missing.

1. Walter E. Disney was born in Chicago Illinois on December 5 1901.
2. On February 22 1950 his famous cartoon *Cinderella* was released.
3. He opened Disneyland in Anaheim California in the late spring of 1955.
4. Disney World in Orlando Florida became the second big amusement park with his name.
5. He created animated shows in May 1964 for the New York World's Fair.

(4) A comma is used after the greeting and the closing in a friendly letter.

The standard form of a friendly letter is shown in this example.

293 Waterway Dr.
Fort Lauderdale,
Florida 33313
December 2, 1980

Dear Jimmy,

Last weekend Uncle Myron took our whole family for a long ride in his power boat. We went out of sight of land. The ocean was pretty rough, and we all had to wear life jackets. I got to steer part of the time.

We could have gone even farther than we did, but Janie began to get sick. Mom made Uncle Myron turn around and come in. I didn't feel sick at all.

Maybe if you can get your mom to let you come over for a weekend, we can go out on the boat. You could tell her it's better than staying around an old apartment.

Sincerely,

Russ

REVIEW EXERCISES for Punctuation come at the end of Chapter 11.

PUNCTUATION

Colons, Hyphens, Apostrophes, Quotation Marks

This chapter presents the additional kinds of inside punctuation that are used to separate the parts of a sentence. Several punctuation marks that are used to enclose groups of words are also discussed.

INSIDE PUNCTUATION

The Colon

11a A colon is used to introduce a list of items.

EXAMPLES   Those jeans come in the following sizes: small, medium, large, and extra large.
These are the only colors: blue, brown, and mahogany.

Use no punctuation after a verb or preposition followed by a list.

EXAMPLES   Effie's best talents were loafing, eating, and sleeping.
No one every heard of a pie made of apples, pickles, mustard, and chestnuts.

11b A colon is used in numerals expressing time.

EXAMPLE   4:25 in the morning (or 4:25 A.M.)

EXERCISE 1 Copy the following six items on your paper. Put in commas and colons where they are needed.

1. There can be no reason Emile for making such an error.
2. Swimming diving and boating kept the young people busy the whole weekend.
3. The adults were too tired to do anything but eat sleep or be in the shade.
4. Name the author who wrote these books *The Three Musketeers The Count of Monte Cristo* and *The Man in the Iron Mask.*
5. Dear Barbara
   Please let me know when you will be able to come for a visit. My mom says you are always welcome.

   Sincerely

   Susan

6. The mail came at 1200 noon today instead of 1130.

The Hyphen

11c **A hyphen is used to connect the parts of certain compound words and word numbers from *twenty-one* to *ninety-nine*.**

EXAMPLES mother-in-law, thirty-two (but not *hundred and one*), pull-ups, the check-out counter

Some compound words do not need a hyphen, for example: *chairperson, midday.* Look in a new dictionary for any word in question.

11d **A hyphen is used to divide words at the end of a line.**

EXAMPLES My dear Watson, the case is ele-
mentary to me.
This man is the victim of a crim-
inal.

Divide words between syllables. Do not divide words in a way that will cause incorrect pronunciation.

WRONG Crime in these communities is asto-
nishing.
RIGHT Crime in these communities is aston-
ishing.

The Apostrophe

11e **An apostrophe is used with nouns to show possession or close relationship.**

See Noun, p. 266

EXAMPLES   This is my aunt's apartment.
Dogs' noses should be cool.
The elm's branches spread wide.

(1) Most singular nouns form the possessive with an apostrophe and an *s*.

EXAMPLES   John's   cat's

(2) A plural noun ending in *s* forms the possessive with an apostrophe only.

EXAMPLES   the ants' nests
some girls' shoes

(3) A plural noun not ending in *s* adds an apostrophe and an *s*.

EXAMPLES   the women's lockers
the children's toys

EXERCISE 2   Number a sheet of paper from 1 to 10. Copy each of the following items and add an apostrophe where it is missing.

1. the clowns face
2. the young mans car
3. the foxs nose
4. many boats sails
5. the horses manes
6. a subways tracks
7. a matchs flame
8. several rabbits tails
9. that shirts buttons
10. womens fashions

11f An apostrophe is used to show that letters have been omitted.

The following examples are *contractions*. They are words that have been put together. One or more letters may be missing from a contraction. An apostrophe shows where these letters are missing.

EXAMPLES   isn't (is not)

don't (do not)
I'm (I am)

She'd (she would)
hasn't (has not)
we'll (we will)

Do not confuse the contraction *it's* and *its* or *who's* and *whose*. When spoken, these words sound alike. But they do not mean the same. *It's* is a contraction of *it is*. *It's* does not show possession.

EXERCISE 3   Number a sheet of paper from 1 to 10. The following sentences contain contractions, but the apostrophes are missing. Next to each number write the contraction or contractions and put in the missing apostrophes.

1. Elmer couldnt make training practice yesterday.
2. Hes been sick.
3. He wont be out today either.
4. He hasnt been looking well all week.
5. I dont know whats the matter.
6. Its not that hes in any pain.
7. Im sure hed like to be ready to perform.

8. Whos going to take his place if hes not well.
9. Wed better get Ziggy ready to go.
10. We dont want to disappoint the other seals.

ENCLOSING PUNCTUATION

Some punctuation marks are used to enclose groups of words. These two main marks are quotation marks (" ") and parentheses ( ).

Quotation Marks

11g Quotation marks are used to enclose a speaker's exact words.

EXAMPLES "Look up," shouted the astronaut.
The passenger thought a moment and asked, "Which way is up?"

11h Quotation marks also use commas to separate them from other parts of the sentence.

When quotation marks begin a sentence, a comma follows them. When quotation marks end a sentence, a comma comes before them. When placed next to each other, the comma always comes just before the quotation marks.

EXAMPLES Barbara yelled, "Get out of the boat!"
"Let's jump," groaned Joanie as she stumbled toward the bow, "before it's too late."

11i A period always goes inside the end quotation marks.

A question mark or an exclamation mark goes inside the quotation marks if the quotation is a question or an exclamation. Otherwise, these marks go outside the quotation marks.

EXAMPLES   The green parrot asked, "What does Polly want?"
The blue parrot answered, "Polly wants a cracker."
Did the blue parrot really say, "Polly wants a cracker"?
It also said, "Now!"

EXERCISE 4   Write the following sentences on a piece of paper. Add the missing quotation marks and commas.

EXAMPLE   Joan said Don't go to that beach tonight.

Joan said, "Don't go to that beach tonight."

1. Why can't I go? Ronny asked.
2. Because she answered I've heard there's a monster there.
3. Pooh Ronny snorted that's the silliest thing I've heard.
4. Joan looked embarrassed and said slowly I just thought you'd like to know.
5. Next time Ronny said fiercely don't bother to try to help!

REVIEW EXERCISE A   Punctuation

All punctuation marks have been left out of the following twenty sentences. Write each sentence on a sheet of paper. Number them in correct order. Put in the missing punctuation.

1. When Halloween came to Clinton Iowa on Oct 30 1979 young people dressed up as ghosts witches and other strange creatures
2. They stopped at one house after another and yelled Trick or treat
3. Did you go out then, too
4. In our town its the custom for some to collect money for UNICEF
5. However many like to collect candy chewing gum fruit or special treats
6. Halloween the time of mystery makes me think of vampires
7. Whats a vampire asked a friend of mine
8. Im not sure I replied but lets look it up
9. Vampires dont exist in real life but people in Europe used to believe they did
10. Here are some facts we found out people thought a vampire slept in its coffin came out at night to drink the blood of human beings and returned to its coffin before daybreak.
11. A vampire has pale skin burning eyes and long sharp teeth
12. A vampires breath smells foul
13. If it gets close enough for you to smell its breath, look out
14. What can you do to save yourself from this vicious blood-hungry demon
15. For one thing wave a bunch of garlic in its face

16. For another try shining a bright steady light in its eyes

17. These are two of the ways to beat off a vampire but they wont stop it forever.

18. Instead somebody must drive a wooden stake through its heart while its asleep in its coffin and then they must bury the demons body at a crossroads

19. Whos brave enough to try asked my friend

20. I cant I answered because Ill be too busy getting fresh batteries for my flashlight digging up some garlic from the garden and sharpening a long wooden stake

REVIEW EXERCISE B   End Punctuation

Write the following sentences on your paper. Put in the necessary marks of end punctuation.

1. Oh My watch stopped

2. What time is it

3. Big Ben is an enormous tower clock in London

4. Many clocks chime every hour

5. A sun dial works best on a sunny day

6. Many people depend on an alarm clock to wake them in time for work

7. Have you ever seen a Braille watch

8. Wow It was really expensive to get the clock fixed

9. Quartz clocks are very accurate

10. Her watch also tells the temperature

UNIT FIVE

AIDS AND ENRICHMENT

Speaking and Listening
Spelling
Sources of Information

SPEAKING AND LISTENING

How you speak and how you listen make a difference in how well you get along with others. If you speak well, others will listen. If you listen well, others will want to talk to you.

No one becomes a good speaker or a good listener just by chance. There are some basic rules to follow. The rules in this chapter can help you become a better speaker and listener.

INFORMAL CONVERSATION

What you say to your family or your friends may not seem very important to you. After all, they know you. You can talk to them any time about almost anything.

The way you speak grows into a set of habits, however. The habits carry over from one conversation to others. There are good habits and bad habits. A good habit in conversation is to *think first, then speak*. Ask yourself what you really mean to say, what you want the other person to hear, and what you want to happen as a result of what you have said.

To develop good speaking habits, follow these simple rules.

12a Think before you speak.

(1) Talk about what will interest your listener.

Too often people talk only about what interests them. Think about what will interest your listeners before you speak. If you do not know, begin by asking a question.

(2) Ask questions to give the other person a chance to talk.

Good conversation means sharing ideas and feelings. This means everyone should have a turn to say something. Listen to yourself to find out how much you talk in a conversation. If you usually talk more than half the time, that may be too much. Ask a question of another person. Then stop talking and listen.

Sometimes if three or four people are in a conversation, one or two do most of the talking. The others may say little. If you see this happening, ask a question of someone who has been silent.

One question may not be enough to bring everyone into the conversation. If it is not, think of another question and ask it.

Here are examples of questions you can ask to help a conversation:

"What do you think about (the topic being discussed)?"
"Do you like _____ ?"
"Have you seen (a show)?"
"Have you been to (a place)?"
"Have you heard (a musical group or piece)?"

(3) Control the sound of your voice.

Taking part in a conversation is not the same as belonging to a cheering section at a basketball game.

Loud and shrill voices are all right for shouting in a crowd. In conversation you should keep control of your voice so that it is pleasant for others to listen to.

12b Speak and listen to others the way you want them to speak and listen to you.

This is the Golden Rule of speaking and listening. It means that you consider another person as important as yourself. If you always speak and listen to another person as you would like to be spoken and listened to, good results will come.

EXERCISE 1   Take the part of the speaker or the listener in one of the following situations.

1. You are sitting with your parent in the waiting room of your dentist. A classmate you know slightly comes in with an adult and sits near you. You start talking to your classmate.

2. You are waiting to see your school counselor about a change in your schedule. A new student sits beside you waiting to see your counselor also. You begin a conversation.

3. During the holidays, a neighbor gives a party for a number of families in the neighborhood. Your parents insist you go with them to the party. At the party, almost everyone is an adult. However, you see someone near your age whom you have seen from a distance in the neighborhood. You talk to that person.

INTRODUCTIONS

Introducing people to each other helps them get to know each other. Learning to make introductions requires a little practice in following some simple rules.

12c Introduce people who do not know each other.

If you know that two people in your group are strangers to each other, introduce them. If you remain silent, it may seem that you do not want to help them get to know each other.

Here are examples of informal introductions:

Look at Christie and say, "Christie, this is Beth Orly."

Then look at Beth and say, "This is Christie Smith."

"Frank, meet Lou Tracy."
"Lou, this is Frank Olsada."

Here are some examples of informal introductions with information added. Information of this kind will often help others to speak freely.

"Jack, meet Mike Donley. He's just moved in next door to me."

"I'd like you to meet Stella Brown. Stella and I went to the movies Saturday afternoon."

"Bob, have you met Bill Blakey? He's great at shooting free throws."

"Marie, I'd like you to meet Juanita Rosario. She plays the clarinet. You ought to hear her."

12d In an introduction, first say the name of the person for whom you wish to show special respect.

Usually, you should show special respect to adults when making introductions. You can show respect by saying the name of the older person first.

EXAMPLES   "Mrs. Gaines, this is my friend Betty Staples."

"Dr. Kondo, I'd like to introduce Dick Shores. He and I are in the same class at school."

12e When you are being introduced, listen closely to the name of the person new to you.

A person's name is important. Remember the name of the person introduced to you. If you do not hear it clearly, ask that it be repeated. Here are some ways of asking:

> "I'm sorry, but I didn't hear your name. What is it again?"
> "I didn't quite hear your name. Would you tell me again, please?"
> "Sorry, I missed your name. Would you tell me again?"
> "Excuse me, but I had trouble hearing your name. Would you repeat it?"

When you hear the person's name, repeat it in a response. Here are some suggested responses.

SEMIFORMAL "How do you do, Mrs. Gaines."
INFORMAL "Hi, Juanita. Good to meet you."
SEMIFORMAL "I'm pleased to meet you, Dr. Kondo."

EXERCISE 2 Take one of the parts in the following situations.

1. A representative from the local Benefit Society calls on your family. The representative is trying to gain your family's cooperation during their annual membership and fund drive. You answer the door. You learn the name of the representative. You introduce the person to members of your family.
2. You and two members of your family get in a long line to buy tickets at a local theater. Behind you come one of your teachers and an adult who is a stranger to you. You introduce everyone.

3. Your uncle and aunt are visiting in your home. A school friend not known to any of your family comes to visit you. You introduce your friend to your parents and uncle and aunt.

FORMAL SPEAKING AND LISTENING

12f Use formal language when speaking to a group.

Making an announcement to a group or giving a report in class calls for formal language. Formal language means choosing your words carefully to avoid using slang. It means delivering them in a way that shows respect for your listeners.

If only one or two people are around to hear you, you need not be very formal. But if a dozen or more people are listening to you, plan your talk carefully. Deliver it correctly.

12g Plan your talk in advance.

Think ahead about what you want to say. It may help to write it out. Then read your words out loud and listen to yourself.

A good way to hear how your voice sounds is to cup your hand behind your ear. This traps extra sounds coming out of your mouth. You hear your words clearly. You nearly become a member of your own audience.

Plan to begin your talk by telling your audience what your topic will be, that is, what the main idea is. End your talk by summing up the most important things you said about the topic. Don't forget to thank your listeners.

Outlining

A good way to keep the order of your points is with an *outline.* A formal outline uses numbers and letters. The first topic or main point is marked with a Roman numeral I. Under it come subtopics or sub-points shown by capital letters A, B, C, and so on. These are indented.

Under each subtopic or sub-point come less important topics or details. These are shown by Arabic numerals 1, 2, 3, and so on. They are indented further.

The outline might look like this:

I. (First topic or main point)
   A. (First subtopic or sub-point)
      1. (First less important detail)
      2. (Second less important detail)
   B. (Second sub-point)
II. (Second topic or main point)
   A. (First subtopic or sub-point of second main point)
   B. (Second subtopic or sub-point of second main point)
III. (Final topic or main point)

Suppose you are to give a talk on the history of the circus. In preparing for your talk you find facts about ancient Roman days, the middle centuries in Europe, and modern times in America. These three main time periods you could put as Points I, II, and III. Under each main point you could put subpoints that relate to the main points. An example follows:

HISTORY OF THE CIRCUS

I. Beginnings in Ancient Rome
   A. Pre-Christian times
      1. Chariot races
      2. Wild animal exhibits
      3. Contests among gladiators
   B. Early Christian times
      1. Wild animals *vs.* Christians
      2. Gladiators *vs.* Christians
II. Growth in Europe
   A. After the fall of Rome
      1. Traveling clowns
      2. Trained animals
   B. During the 1700's
      1. Astley, trick riding in England
      2. Franconi family of Italy
III. Recent developments in America
   A. During the 1800's
      1. Small groups of traveling performers
      2. Phineas T. Barnum
   B. Modern days
      1. A few small, touring shows
      2. The huge Ringling Bros., Barnum & Bailey Circus

Preparing Your Report

If you are going to give a report to a class, here are six important steps to take in preparing your report.

1. Choose a topic you know something about or can research.

2. Choose a topic that will interest most of your listeners.
3. Find out more information than you can use in your report.
4. Select the information that will mean the most to your listeners.
5. Organize your information in three main parts: the opening, the body, the ending.
6. Write out your report or write notes to remind you of the most important points.

Delivering Your Report

12h **Deliver your talk the way you would want to listen to it.**

(1) Speak clearly.

During your talk, speak to your listeners just the way you would want to be spoken to. No one in an audience likes to have to strain to hear the speaker's words. Pronounce your words carefully. Use enough volume so that those in the back of the room can hear what you say.

(2) Speak to your listeners.

Look at the faces of your listeners as often as you can. Let them know by your eyes that you are talking to them. It is all right to look at your notes from time to time. Avoid burying your face behind your notes or looking always at your feet, however.

(3) Remain still except to make an important point.

Do not wiggle, sway, or twist your hands. Motions like these catch the eyes of your listeners. Their attention is drawn away from what you are saying.

(4) Look pleasant.

Try to appear pleasing to your listeners. You may be feeling uncomfortable. That is no reason to make your listeners feel uncomfortable, too, however. Smile once in a while—at least at the beginning and end of your report. Be sure your clothes do not look sloppy. Help your listeners be pleased with what you offer.

(5) Avoid useless sounds and words.

Sounds such as *"ah"* and *"um"* are not words. If you use them in your talk, your listeners will have trouble paying attention.

Words repeated too often begin to lose meaning. *"I mean"* or *"you know"* add nothing when they come in almost every sentence.

Say what you want your listeners to hear. Make your words useful, not useless.

12i Listen to a talk the way you would want others to listen if you were giving it.

Follow the Golden Rule for listening. Pay attention to the speaker. This is what you would want your listeners to do if you were giving the talk.

Do nothing that might interrupt. Opening and closing a book, scuffing your feet, turning to look around the room—all can cause interruptions. Perhaps the worst interruption is talking while the speaker is talking. Avoid doing anything which will disturb the speaker or the other listeners.

REVIEW EXERCISE A   Outlining

Choose one of the following titles as a topic for a formal talk. Find out information about your topic. Write an outline of at least three main points. List two or three sub-points under each main point.

A plan for better student government
Growing a house plant
Simple ways to save energy in the home
A plan for saving money
How to study in a crowded home
Ways to save our (choose a species of animal,
    such as seals, eagles, or others)
Ways to save our (choose an important kind of
    plant)
The value of cosmetics
The value of team sports
The value of individual sports

REVIEW EXERCISE B   Preparing a Formal Talk

Prepare a formal talk on a topic in Exercise A. Or choose a topic that is similar. Write out your talk or write notes. Be prepared to give your talk to others in your class.

SPELLING

Correct spelling is just one of the many basics in English. But it is an important one. This is so whether you write a great deal or only a little. Your spelling shows up right away.

To be a good speller you need practice. Very few people become good spellers without it. Even the people who write dictionaries needed practice to learn how to spell.

Practice leads to the building of habits. Once you build good spelling habits, you find it easier to learn to spell by the rules.

This chapter will help you be a better speller.

RULES FOR GOOD SPELLING

13a Develop basic spelling habits.

Spelling correctly is not always easy. A little care and effort will pay off for you, however.

(1) Keep a list of troublesome words.

Start a list if you have none. Write down each word that gives you trouble. List the words you have used and misspelled. Keep your list in your notebook. When you learn to spell a word on your list, put a check beside it. See how many words you can check off each week.

(2) Study the hard parts of words.

Look over your list and underline the parts of words that cause you the most trouble. Usually only one or two letters in a word cause trouble. For example, the word *believe* is often misspelled. Only the letters **ie** in the middle cause the trouble.

See Master
Spelling List,
pp. 233–235

**(3) See each syllable. Say each syllable.
Write each syllable.**

A *syllable* is made up of one main vowel sound. It may have one or two consonant sounds with it, or it may have none.

Pronounce each word carefully syllable by syllable. See the group of letters in each syllable as you hear yourself say it. Write each syllable as you say it.

EXAMPLES

BEAU-TI-FUL
(beautiful)

This word has three syllables. The first syllable is hard to spell. The other two are easy. Look closely at the first syllable. It has three vowel letters but only one vowel sound—*yoo*. Say each syllable and write each one.

TUES-DAY   This word has two syllables.
(Tuesday)   Only the first syllable is hard
                  to spell. It starts with a
                  capital letter. It has the two
                  vowel letters **u** and **e**.

VI-TA-MIN   This word has three syllables.
(vitamin)   Only the last one causes
                  trouble.

(4) Use a dictionary.

See Sources of
Information,
pp. 237–242 A dictionary has the correct spellings of words. Be sure you start with the correct first letter when you look up a word. You will have problems if you confuse such words as *affect* and *effect*.

13b Learn basic spelling rules.

Rules for spelling can be helpful, but they are only guides. Almost every rule has an exception. Learn each rule and how it applies. Then learn the exception to the rule.

(1) Most nouns form the plural by adding the letters *s* or *es*.

EXAMPLES
Nouns that add **s**:   banana, banana**s**
                           duck, duck**s**
                           hat, hat**s**
                           lemon, lemon**s**
                           night, night**s**

Nouns that add **es:**   box, box**es**
                             match, match**es**
                             sash, sash**es**
                             hiss, hiss**es**

Hint: Add an **es** to form the plural if the singular noun ends in **ch, s, sh, x,** or **z.** Otherwise, add only an **s.**

Compound nouns form their plurals in special ways. Often you will want to use a dictionary to be sure what the plural form is.

EXAMPLES mother-in-law, mothers-in-law
                     sail boat, sail boat**s**
                     jackknife, jackkniv**es**

EXERCISE 1 Number a sheet of paper from 1 to 10. Write the plural of the following nouns.

1. horse
2. push
3. pot
4. six
5. sock
6. suitcase
7. clutch
8. lass
9. birch
10. berth

(2) **Nouns ending in the letter _y_ following a consonant change the _y_ to _i_ and add _es_ to form the plural.**

EXAMPLES county, count**ies**   puppy, pupp**ies**

If a vowel comes before the final **y,** just add **s.**

EXAMPLES boy, boy**s**   monkey, monkey**s**

EXERCISE 2   Number a sheet of paper from 1 to 6. Write the plural of the following nouns.

1. baby   3. key   5. turkey
2. toy   4. lady   6. chimney

(3)   Most nouns ending in the letter *f* add *s* to form the plural.

> EXAMPLES   puff, puffs
> whiff, whiffs

(4)   Some nouns ending in the letter *f* or the letters *fe* change the *f* to *v* and add *es* or *s*.

> EXAMPLES   knife, kni**ves**
> wolf, wol**ves**

(5)   Most nouns ending in the letter *o* following a vowel add *s* to form the plural.

> EXAMPLES   studio, studios
> rodeo, rodeos

(6)   Most nouns ending in the letter *o* following a consonant add *es* to form the plural.

> EXAMPLES   potato, potatoes
> echo, echoes

(7)   Almost all musical terms ending in the letter *o* add only *s* to form the plural.

> EXAMPLES   solo, solos
> alto, altos

(8) A few nouns are irregular and form the plural
without adding *s* or *es*. Some change
spelling. Some do not.

EXAMPLES   woman, wom**en**   goose, g**ee**se
                  child, child**ren**   mouse, **mi**ce
                  deer, deer

EXERCISE 3   Number a sheet of paper from 1 to
25. Following are twenty-five singular nouns. Each
one follows a rule given earlier. Write each word in
its plural form. You may use a dictionary to check
your work.

EXAMPLE   catch

catches

1. patch
2. vine
3. beauty
4. ration
5. wolf
6. chill
7. child
8. entry
9. waltz
10. woman
11. duty
12. belief
13. pass
14. fox
15. monkey
16. kiss
17. boo
18. piccolo
19. donkey
20. mystery
21. tomato
22. switch
23. tooth
24. fish
25. laugh

Prefixes

(9) A new word may be formed by adding a
prefix to a root.

Some words can add letters at the front. An
example is the word *run* which can be made into

the word *rerun*. The letters **re** are called a *prefix*.
Run is the root. Examples of prefixes are **dis, in,**
and **mis.** Most prefixes are not words by themselves. Some roots are not words by themselves.

EXAMPLES	PREFIX	ROOT	NEW WORD
	dis	appear	disappear
		respect	disrespect
		satisfy	dissatisfy
	in	direct	indirect
		legal	illegal
			(**in** changes to **il** to match the first letter of *legal*)
		mature	immature
			(**in** changes to **im** to match the first letter of *mature*)
	mis	lead	mislead
		spell	misspell
	ex	plain	explain
	pro	-nounce	pronounce
	un	do	undo
		kind	unkind

EXERCISE 4   Number a sheet of paper from 1 to 5.
There are five prefixes in column 1. Next to each
number write a word that can be made by adding a
prefix from column 1 with a root in column 2.

1	2
mis	mediate
im	turb
un	spent
re	turn
dis	lead

Suffixes

Sometimes a word adds letters after it to form a new word. An example is the word *quick* which can be made into the words *quickly* or *quickness*. The letters **ly** and **ness** are called *suffixes*.

(10) A new word may be formed by adding a suffix to another word.

EXAMPLES   faint, faint**ly**
dark, dark**ness**

Root words already ending in **y** usually change the **y** to **i** before adding the suffix **ly** or **ness**.

EXAMPLES   happy, happ**ily**
silly, sill**iness**

(11) Most words ending in *e* drop the *e* when adding a suffix that begins with a vowel.

EXAMPLES   please, pleas**ing**
move, mov**able**

However, most words ending in **ce** or **ge** keep the **e** when adding a suffix that begins with an **a** or an **o**.

replace, replace**able**
manage, manage**able**

(12) **Most words ending in *e* keep it when adding a suffix that begins with a consonant.**

EXAMPLES   arrange, arrange**ment**
sincere, sincere**ly**

(13) **Most words ending in *y* following a consonant change the *y* to *i* when adding a suffix that does not begin with *i*.**

EXAMPLES   cry, cr**ied**
beauty, beaut**iful**

(14) **One-syllable words ending in a single consonant following a single vowel double the consonant before adding the suffixes ed, ing, or er.**

EXAMPLES   tip, tip**ping**
slap, slap**ping**

EXERCISE 5   Number a sheet of paper from 1 to 20. For each following item there is a word and a suffix. Write the correct spelling of each word with its suffix added.

EXAMPLE   sloppy + ness

sloppiness

1. slow + ly
2. happy + ness
3. broad + ly
4. heavy + ly
11. place + ment
12. nice + ly
13. merry + ment
14. fry + ed

5. light + ly   15. bare + ly
6. bathe + ing   16. move + ment
7. tap + ing   17. rise + ing
8. wear + able   18. pad + ing
9. trace + able   19. lace + ing
10. prod + ing   20. pit + ing

SOUNDS OF LETTERS

Many words have parts that sound the same but are spelled differently. An example of this is the sound of **s** in the beginning of the words *sit* and *city*.

Another example is the sound of **k**. In *kite* it is a **k**. In *come* it is represented by a **c**. In *chorus* it is represented by a **ch**.

13c Learn the different ways of spelling single sounds.

Here are some common sounds that may be spelled with different letters of the alphabet. Study them so that you become familiar with useful spelling patterns.

SOUND	EXAMPLES OF SPELLING PATTERNS
ch (as in *chair*)	**ch**air, wat**ch**, ques**ti**on, pic**t**ure
f (as in *fun*)	**f**un, pu**ff**, lau**gh**, **ph**one
g (as in *get*)	**g**et, **gh**ost
j (as in *judge*)	**j**udge, ma**g**ic, bri**dge**, sol**di**er
k (as in *kite*)	**k**ite, **c**at, **ch**oir, ba**ck**
m (as in *mat*)	**m**at, clim**b**, ham**m**ock, cal**m**

n (as in *not*)	not, **kn**ow, wi**nn**er, **gn**at, **pn**eumonia
sh (as in *shame*)	**sh**ame, mi**ss**ion, **s**ure, sta**ti**on, ma**ch**ine
t (as in *tell*)	**t**ell, walk**ed**
z (as in *zig-zag*)	**z**ig-**z**ag, doe**s**, sci**ss**ors
a (as in *ate*)	**a**te, **ai**d, br**ea**k
e (as in *be*)	b**e**, s**ee**, s**ea**t, p**eo**ple, rel**ie**f, rec**ei**ve, ma**chi**ne, funn**y**
i (as in *pipe*)	p**i**pe, p**ie**, b**uy**, tr**y**, **eye**
i (as in *it*)	**i**t, b**u**sy, b**ui**ld, w**o**men
o (as in *open*)	**o**pen, l**oa**d, t**oe**, b**ow**l, s**ew**
u (as in *united*)	**u**nited, b**eau**ty, p**ew**, y**ou**
u (as in *rule*)	r**u**le, s**ui**t, tr**oo**p, gr**ou**p, thr**ew**, m**o**ve

HOMONYMS

Words called homonyms sound alike but are not spelled the same way. Some examples are *peace* and *piece,* or *tail* and *tale.* Take special care as you spell words that sound alike. Learn which spelling goes with the meaning you have in mind.

13d Learn which spelling of a homonym belongs with the meaning you want.

HOMONYMS	MEANINGS
already	earlier, in the past
all ready	(two words) completed, ready
capital	a government city, a large letter
capitol	the building of government
hear	to listen

here	in this spot
its	belonging to it
it's	it is (a contraction)
passed	went by (a verb)
past	of an earlier time
pair	two of anything
pare	to cut
pear	a fruit
their	showing belonging to them
there	in that place
they're	they are (a contraction)

REVIEW EXERCISE A   Plural Nouns

Number a sheet of paper from 1 to 15. Write the plural form of each of the following nouns.

1.	bunch	6.	dish	11.	shelf
2.	crash	7.	peach	12.	echo
3.	body	8.	solo	13.	mouse
4.	worry	9.	fox	14.	toy
5.	key	10.	lady	15.	child

REVIEW EXERCISE B   Prefixes and Suffixes

The following ten words have prefixes or suffixes in them. Number a sheet of paper from 1 to 10. Write the root of each word in the list.

EXAMPLE   **recap**

cap

1. happily   6. helpful
2. courageous   7. hopping
3. impossible   8. rising
4. disappear   9. disinterest
5. management   10. movable

REVIEW EXERCISE C   Rhyming Spelling

A word is missing from each of the following sentences. Only its first letter is given. The missing word rhymes with or sounds like the word in parentheses, but is a different word. Number a sheet of paper from 1 to 10. Next to each number write the word that belongs in the blank. The first one is done for you as an example.

EXAMPLE Each p_____ in the church had a
         name on it. (you)

pew

1. Each p_____ in the church had a name on it. (you)
2. She l_____ at the jokes. (raft)
3. All the p_____ in the town voted. (steeple)
4. The weatherperson looked for a b_____ in the clouds. (cake)
5. The mountaineers tried to c_____ the cliff. (lime)
6. They stopped when they got t_____ . (care)
7. The days p_____ one by one. (cast)
8. The snail lost i_____ shell. (pits)
9. Enjoy a fresh p_____ after lunch. (leech)
10. Can you h_____ any noise now? (deer)

MASTER SPELLING LIST

The following list includes words frequently misspelled. Your study of this list should be by groups of words. Practice spelling ten or twenty at a time. Be sure you also know the meaning of each word. Where necessary, look up words in a dictionary.

From time to time, review words you have misspelled at an earlier time. By doing this you help to keep their spellings clear in your mind.

The hard parts of words are printed in darker ink. The darker letters will help you pay close attention to the parts often misspelled.

absence
accidentally
accompany
accuracy
achieve
acquire
across
actually
administration
admittance
advertisement
afraid
agriculture
aisle
altar/alter
amateur
annually
apology
apparent
appearance
appreciate
approach
approval

argue
argument
arrangement
athletic
attendance
authority
available

beginning
behavior
believe
benefit
buried
business

calendar
campaign
capital/capitol
cemetery
certificate
character
chief
Christian
choice

choose/chose
clothes
color
column
commercial
committee
competitor
completely
concentrate
confidential
confusion
conscience
conscious
controlled
cooperate
correspondence
courageous
criticism
criticize
cruelly
curiosity
curious
cylinder

deceive
decision
dependent
describe
despair
desperate
difference
dining
dinner
disappearance
disappoint
discipline
duplicate

eager
easily
effect
eighth
eligible
embarrass
emphasize
encouragement
entirely
entrance
environment
equipped
escape
especially
exaggerate
excellent
exciting
exercise
existence
expense
experiment
extremely

fantasy
fashionable
favorite

field
finally
financial
foreign
forty
fortunately
forward
fourth
friend

genius
government
gracious
grammar
guarantee
guess
gymnasium

happened
happiness
hear/here
heavily
height
hopeless
hospital
humor
humorous
hungrily

ignorance
imagine
immediately
increase
indefinite
individually
influence
ingredient
innocence
insurance
intelligence

interference
interrupt

jealous
judgment

knowledge

laboratory
laborer
laid
leisure
lessen/lesson
license
likely
listener
lively
loneliness
loose/lose/loss
luxury

magazine
maintenance
manufacturer
marriage
meant
mechanic
medical
medicine
merchandise
miniature
minimum
minute
mischief
moral/morale
muscle
mysterious

naturally
niece
ninety
noticeable

obstacle
occasionally
occurrence
offensive
official
often
omission
omit
once
operate
opponent
opportunity
optimist
orchestra
organization
originally

paid
parallel
particular
passed/past
peace/piece
peaceful
peculiar
performance
permanent
perspiration
persuade
physical
picnicking
pleasant
politician
possession
practically
practice
preferred
prejudice
preparation
presence
pressure
privilege

probably
procedure
proceed
psychology
pursuit

quiet
quite

realize
really
receipt
recognize
recommend
referred
relieve
religious
removal
repetition
resistance
resource
responsibility
restaurant
rhythm
ridiculous

sacrifice
safety
satisfied
scarcity
scene
schedule
scholar
scissors
seize
separate
similar
simplify
sincerely
skiing
sophomore
source

sponsor
straight
strength
stretch
strictly
stubborn
substitute
succeed
successful
sufficient
summary
surprise
suspense
swimming
synonym

tendency
therefore
thorough
though
thoughtful
tragedy
transferred
tremendous
truly

unanimous
unnecessary
useful
useless
usually

vacuum
valuable
various

weather/whether
weird
whole/hole

yield

CHAPTER

14

SOURCES OF INFORMATION

Where do you go when you want to find out about something? Maybe you want to know little things such as how a compass works or how a hummingbird flies. Maybe you want to know about big things such as how much water there is on the earth, or how much heat the sun gives off every day. Or maybe you only want to know what words to use to say something.

This chapter tells you about places to go to find out things. It tells you the best ways to make use of sources of information.

TEXTBOOKS

Most textbooks have basic parts that make them easy to use. These parts can be found in the textbook you are reading now.

The *front cover* usually lists the title and the

author. The *back edge,* which is called the *"spine,"* often repeats that information and also gives the name of the publisher. Information on the spine makes it easy to identify any book when several are stacked together.

The *inside cover* is also called the *"end paper."* In this book it is used to show information about the history of the English language. Some books leave the end papers blank.

The *title page* repeats information from the cover. The *copyright page* is usually the back of the title page. It gives the date of publication and tells who owns the rights to the book. The *introduction* or *preface* explains what the book is about and how it can be used. It may also tell why certain features are included.

The *table of contents* lists chapter titles and contents by page numbers. The *text* contains the major contents of the book. The *index* is an alphabetic listing of the main topics found in the book, with page numbers. The *glossary* defines many terms used in the book and often gives examples. Some books have no glossary, or it may be combined with the index.

THE DICTIONARY

Dictionaries give information about words and their uses. You use words every day. Sometimes you use them well. Other times you may wish you used them better. A dictionary can help you use more words in better ways.

14a Learn how a dictionary can help you.

(1) Words are listed alphabetically.

When you know the kinds of information that can be found in a dictionary, you will find it a very useful book. All dictionaries list words in alphabetical order. Words that begin with the same letter, such as *club, coat,* and *cross,* are listed in order by their second letters, for example, **l, o,** and **r.** Words that have the same first few letters like *hamburger, hammer,* and *hamper* are listed by the next letter that is different, for example, **b, m,** and **p.**

EXERCISE 1 Number a sheet of paper from 1 to 12. Write the following words in alphabetical order.

join	living	main
melt	master	help
half	just	joke
little	large	have

(2) Guide words at the top of each page show which words are on that page.

To make it easy to find a word, the dictionary puts two guide words at the top of every page. The guide word on the left is the same as the first word listed on that page. The guide word on the right is the same as the last word on the page. The rest of the words on that page are alphabetized.

Suppose *shackle* is the guide word on the left and *shake* is the guide word on the right, for example. You know that any word on that page begins with the letters **sha.** You also know that the *fourth* letter of any word on this page cannot come before **c** in the alphabet or after **k**. You can expect to find words with the *fourth* letter **d, f,** or **g,** like *shady, shaft,* and *shag.*

| Bering Sea | 67 | bestrew | **B** |

Ber·ing Sea [bâr′ing *or* bir′ing] A part of the northern Pacific Ocean between Alaska and Siberia.
Bering Strait The narrow waterway which connects the Bering Sea to the Arctic Ocean.
berke·li·um [bûrk′lē·əm] *n.* An unstable radioactive element.
Ber·lin [bər·lin′] *n.* A city in east central Germany, the former capital of Germany. It is now divided into **East Berlin,** the capital of East Germany, and **West Berlin,** associated with West Germany.
Ber·mu·da [bər·myōō′də] *n.* A group of British islands in the western Atlantic Ocean.
Bermuda shorts Shorts that reach down to just above the knees, worn by men and women.
Bern or **Berne** [bûrn *or* bern] *n.* The capital of Switzerland, in the west central part.
ber·ry [ber′ē] *n., pl.* **ber·ries,** *v.* **ber·ried, ber·ry·ing 1** *n.* A small, pulpy fruit containing many seeds, as the raspberry. **2** *v.* To gather berries. **3** *n.* Any fleshy fruit enclosed in a soft skin, as the banana.
ber·serk [bûr′sûrk *or* bar·sûrk′] *adj.* In a frenzy of wild rage: The wounded elephant was *berserk.*
berth [bûrth] **1** *n.* A space for sleeping on a ship, train, or airplane. **2** *n.* A place in which a ship may anchor or dock. **3** *v.* To put into or provide with a berth. **4** *n.* A job or position: He found a *berth* as a TV announcer. — **give a wide berth to** To keep safely out of the way of; to *give a wide berth to* a passing truck.
ber·yl [ber′al] *n.* A mineral of great hardness. Some varieties, as the aquamarine and emerald, are used as gems.

4 *prep.* Other than; apart from: I care for nothing *besides* this.
be·siege [bi·sēj′] *v.* **be·sieged, be·sieg·ing 1** To seek to capture by surrounding and wearing down resistance: to *besiege* the castle. **2** To crowd around: to *besiege* a movie star. **3** To bother; harass: to *besiege* a teacher with questions. — **be·sieg′er** *n.*
be·smear [bi·smir′] *v.* To smear over; sully.
be·smirch [bi·smûrch′] *v.* To soil; stain.
be·som [bē′zəm] *n.* A bundle of twigs used as a broom.
be·sot·ted [bi·sot′id] *adj.* Dull or stupefied, as from being foolishly in love or drunk.
be·sought [bi·sôt′] Alternative past tense and past participle of BESEECH.
be·spat·ter [bi·spat′ər] *v.* To cover or soil by spattering, as with mud or paint.
be·speak [bi·spēk′] *v.* **be·spoke** [bi·spōk′] or **be·spo·ken** [bi·spō′kən], **be·speak·ing 1** To ask for or order in advance: He had *bespoken* two seats for the play. **2** To show or indicate; signify: Your manners *bespeak* a good upbringing.
Bes·se·mer process [bes′ə·mər] A process of making steel, in which a blast of air is forced through molten iron to burn out carbon and impurities.
best [best] **1** Superlative of GOOD, WELL. **2** *adj.* Superior to all others; most excellent: I want to buy the *best* wrist watch in the store. **3** *adv.* In the most excellent way: Which watch keeps time *best?* **4** *n.* The best person, thing, part, etc.: If this watch is the *best,* I'll buy it. **5** *adj.* Most favorable; advantageous: Noon will be the *best* time to start our trip. **6** *adj.* Most; largest: He spent the *best* part of his lunch hour reading. **7** *adv.* To the greatest degree; most completely:

EXERCISE 2   Number a sheet of paper from 1 to 8. Suppose the guide words at the top of a dictionary page are *tattoo* and *teaspoon.* Eight of the following words are listed on that page. The others are not. Write the words you could find on that page.

tear	tattletale	taunt
teacup	taught	tax
teenage	team	tee
taste	tease	teapot

(3) Words are spelled by syllables.

Every dictionary word is spelled out by syllables. Perhaps you know how to spell the first syllable in a word but are unsure about other letters.

See Syllable, p. 272

You can usually find the word just by knowing its first syllable.

If you look for a word in one part of a dictionary and can't find it, perhaps it is spelled differently than it looks. Check the list of sounds and spellings in Chapter 13, p. 229, and try again.

If a word has other forms, such as a plural, you can find the spelling of those forms in a dictionary.

EXERCISE 3 Number a sheet of paper from 1 to 10. The following words have misspellings in them, but the first syllable is correctly spelled. Look up each word in a dictionary. Write each word on your paper. Spell each one correctly and break it into syllables.

EXAMPLE personible

per- son- a- ble

1. shovelfull
2. proprieter
3. neckercheif
4. loyelty
5. irigate
6. brutel
7. enimy
8. disposel
9. criticle
10. unemployement

(4) The pronunciation of every word is given.

Dictionaries tell how to pronounce, or say, words by showing their sounds through a special system of marks. Not all dictionaries use the same system, but every dictionary explains its system, usually in the front section. Most dictionaries repeat the basic pronunciation system every pair of pages. Be sure to check the pronunciation system of the dictionary you use. Knowing the system will help you pronounce words correctly.

ber·ry [ber′ē] *n.*, *pl.* **ber·ries,** *v.* **ber·ried, ber·ry·ing 1** *n.* A small, pulpy fruit containing many seeds, as the raspberry. **2** *v.* To gather berries. **3** *n.* Any fleshy fruit enclosed in a soft skin, as the banana.

(5) The part of speech of every word is given.

Usually the part of speech of a word is shown following its pronunciation. If a word can be used as more than one part of speech, this also will be shown.

(6) Various meanings of words are given.

Each meaning of a word in a dictionary is numbered. The meaning you want is the one that fits best in the sentence where you first found the word.

Suppose you come across the word *scene* in this sentence: *Ted's little brother really made a scene in the market yesterday.* You may not be sure what the word *scene* means in this sentence. For a moment you might think it means the scenery in a movie or television show. A dictionary will give several numbered meanings for *scene.* One of them fits best in that sentence. It is "a show of bad temper." The sentence means that Ted's brother showed bad temper.

EXERCISE 4 Following are six sentences with special words underlined. Number a sheet of paper from 1 to 6. Use a dictionary to find the best meaning for each underlined word. Write the meaning for each word.

EXAMPLE   Peter's play was a hit.

a great success

1. Sarah Dipple runs her own business.
2. The evening newspaper will run the story.
3. Our gas pipe runs from this corner to the middle of the street.
4. All her money will pass to her daughter one day.
5. Snow had fallen all night on the pass.
6. Jane had a pass to the theater.

THE LIBRARY

4b **Learn how to use the sources of information in a library.**

(1) The librarian.

The most valuable source of information in a library is the librarian. He or she can help you quickly find the information you want.

Do not depend upon the librarian to tell you what you can and should learn for yourself about library resources. Learn what sources of information a library can offer. Learn how to use those sources of information.

(2) Books of fiction.

Stories made up by authors come under the heading of fiction. These stories are often very interesting, but they are not true. You can find books of fiction on shelves in one part of the library. Fiction books are in alphabetical order according to the last names of the authors.

You will see books by the same author next to each other. A library may have three books by Scott O'Dell: *The Black Pearl, The Dark Canoe,* and *The King's Fifth.* These books would be together in alphabetical order by the first letters in the main words in the titles: *Black, Dark,* and *Kings.*

(3) Books of nonfiction.

Nonfiction books give information about the real world. Anything you may want to read about is probably in some nonfiction book. Every year thousands of nonfiction books are published. They present more facts and ideas than can be counted. How does one keep track of all these books with all this information?

The answer is in the Dewey Decimal System. This system is used by most American libraries to divide nonfiction books by subjects or topics. The Dewey Decimal System has ten major subject divisions. Each subject division has ten subdivisions. Each subdivision has ten more subdivisions. These smaller subdivisions are needed to include all the nonfiction books published. Each division and subdivision has its own number.

THE DEWEY DECIMAL SYSTEM

Book Numbers	Subjects
000-099	General works (reference materials such as encyclopedias)
100-199	Philosophy (the ideas people have about the truth)
200-299	Religion (peoples' beliefs and faiths, including mythology)
300-399	Social sciences (government, the law, financial ideas, and others)
400-499	Language (dictionaries and other books about words and meanings)
500-599	Science
600-699	Technology (agriculture, aviation, engineering, and others)
700-799	The Arts (art, architecture, dance, painting, music, and others)
800-899	Literature (plays, television scripts, poetry, and books about literature)
900-999	History (information about the past, biographies, and travel books)

If a new nonfiction book is published about space science, for example, it belongs in the 500-599 division. Another book about the travels of a famous explorer belongs in the 900-999 division. For every kind of nonfiction book there is a Dewey decimal number.

EXERCISE 5 Following are descriptions of some new books. Number a sheet of paper from 1 to 6. Next to each number write the range of Dewey decimal numbers that the book would belong in.

EXAMPLE a book about a trip to Ceylon

900-999

1. a book about the religious practices in Iran
2. a book about the unusual shapes and colors of certain insects
3. a book telling of a climb up Mt. Everest
4. a book about the life of Fred Astaire, the dancer
5. a book forecasting the problems of making money in the 1990's
6. a book of reviews of the best TV shows of the 1970's

(4) The card catalog.

There is a card in the card catalog for every book a library has. Cards are kept within easy reach in drawers in a library cabinet. The card catalog cabinet holds three kinds of cards.

Author cards. These cards list every library book by its author. They are alphabetized by the authors' last names.

Title cards. These cards list every book by its title. They are alphabetized by the first main word.

Subject cards. These cards are alphabetized by subject. Each card gives the book's title, its author, its publisher, and something about its contents. Subject cards are for nonfiction books.

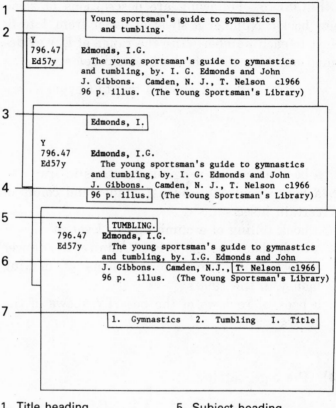

1. Title heading
2. Call number
3. Author
4. Book's physical description

5. Subject heading
6. Publisher, publication date
7. Other headings under
    which the book is listed.

The Dewey decimal number for a book is printed on the card in the upper left corner. Other information on the card gives the number of pages in the book, the number of illustrations, and the date it was published.

(5) Reference works.

Encyclopedias provide some information about nearly all subjects. Most encyclopedias list subjects alphabetically. An article about a subject such as *turtles* will tell what turtles are, the kinds of turtles known, and their life habits. Some encyclopedias include pictures, maps, charts, and graphs to illustrate their subjects. Often at the end of an article there will be a list of books that have more special information about the subject.

Atlases contain maps and written information about what the maps show. Additional information may be found about population, climate, ocean or wind currents, natural resources, and other facts about regions of the world.

Almanacs list facts about all sorts of things. Some of the things that are found in almanacs are as follows:

> sports records
> important events of the year
> population figures
> financial figures
> weather information

Usually almanacs are published every year. This means they contain recent information. The information is not always in alphabetical order. An almanac's alphabetical index helps you find the information you want, however.

(6) Periodicals.

A periodical is any printed material published regularly, such as a magazine or journal. It may appear once a day or only once every few months. Because it is published often, a periodical contains up-to-date information and ideas.

Most libraries subscribe to various periodicals. So many periodicals are published during a year, a library cannot be expected to have them all.

The leading periodicals, which are almost all magazines, are listed in a single index. This index is called the *Readers' Guide to Periodical Literature.* The *Readers' Guide* is issued twenty-two times a year. It lists articles that appear in more than one hundred periodicals in the United States.

Every article is indexed in alphabetical order according to the subject and the author. Abbreviations make it possible to include much information about each article. A key to the abbreviations is in each *Readers' Guide.*

Following is part of a page from the *Readers' Guide.* It shows the kinds of information to be found in it.

> MUSIC, Electronic
> Marshall's Fragility Cycles; sonic performance environments. J. La Barbara. Hi Fi 27:MA15 My '77
> Tudor at The Kitchen; six-day series of electronic music. J. La Barbara. il por Hi Fi 27: MA14-15 My '77
> MUSIC, Latin American
> Music. See issues of Américas
> MUSIC, Modern. See Music
> MUSIC, Spanish American. See Music, Latin American
> MUSIC and literature
> Zeroing in; adaptation of Kirchner's opera Lily from S. Bellow's Henderson, the rain king. H. Heinsheimer. il por Opera N 41:12-15 Ap 16 '77
> MUSIC and religion. See Religion and music

(7) Audio-visual materials.

Sometimes a library will keep recordings and filmstrips on file. It may also have other audiovisual material available.

Check with the librarian to learn what audiovisual material your library contains.

A BASIC LIST OF CONTENTS OF THE LIBRARY

Almanacs: A yearly calendar of facts and events, especially ones about nature, such as weather predictions and the first day of spring.

Atlases: Books of maps, often with written information about places shown on the maps.

Audio-visual materials: Audio recordings on disks, tapes, or cassettes; filmstrips; motion picture film; prints; microfilm; video recordings.

Bibliographies: Lists of books, usually alphabetized by titles, by authors, or by subjects, including information about publishers. An *annotated bibliography* includes comments about the contents of the listed books.

Books

   Fiction: Novels and long or short stories made up by authors.

   Nonfiction: Autobiographies, biographies, accounts of instruction such as cookbooks.

Collected works: Plays, poems, songs, musical pieces, scripts of television or other shows, art reproductions, and photographs.

Dictionaries: Alphabetical listings of words and names with definitions, pronunciations, and related information.

Encyclopedias: Books of one or several volumes containing general information about a broad range of topics, alphabetically arranged.

Indexes: Alphabetical listings of topics, names, or other subject matter.

Pamphlets: Paper-covered sets of printed sheets containing nonfiction information.

Periodicals: Magazines or journals published regularly such as once a week or every month.

OTHER SOURCES OF INFORMATION

14c Learn to use other sources of information.

Often people in your school and community can provide you with special information. This information may not be available from other sources. Historical information, for example, about your school or the area where you live may not be written down. Yet someone may know it and be ready to share it with you.

Local government officials can often supply special information of value and interest. Suppose you want to know the local laws about keeping pets. Can you keep a giraffe in your backyard? A local government official probably can give you that information.

Agencies of your state and of the federal government will provide information relating to thousands of subjects. The various departments in your state and federal government maintain records on a regular basis. By writing to the head of a governmental department, you can usually find out what you want to know.

Businesses sometimes make available printed information about their activities or those of the field in which they specialize. You can find out this information by writing directly to a company.

REVIEW EXERCISE A   Alphabetical Order

Number a sheet of paper from 1 to 12. Write the following words on your paper. Put them in alphabetical order.

sun	wrap	trap
temper	skull	under
shingle	rescue	tumble
render	singe	roast

REVIEW EXERCISE B   Guide Words

The guide words at the top of a dictionary page are *idol* and *illuminate*. Only eight of the following words will be found on that page. Number a sheet of paper from 1 to 8. Write the words you would find on that page.

igloo	idiot	illustrate
illegal	iguana	ignition
image	if	ill
idle	ignite	ignore

REVIEW EXERCISE C   Spelling Words Correctly

Number a sheet of paper from 1 to 8. The following words have misspellings in the middle or at the end. Use a dictionary to help you correct the misspellings. Spell each one correctly on your paper. Break each word into syllables.

EXAMPLE   annuel

an- nu- al

1. permenant
2. restrick
3. medacine
4. laterel
5. harmoney
6. fragence
7. dependance
8. benifit

GLOSSARY

This glossary lists special terms that appear in the text. Most terms are defined here. Those terms not defined are cross-referenced to other terms with definitions. Wherever examples will help, they are provided.

References to parts of the text appear with many terms in this glossary. The text treats these terms more fully.

Adjective   A word that describes a noun. See **1g**.

It was an *ugly* creature.

The *old* lady lived in a *smelly old* shoe.

An adjective helps *compare things*. Most adjectives change form to show comparison. See **1h**.

That person is a *short* giant.

I've never seen a *shorter* giant.

She's probably the *shortest* giant in the world.

Adverb   A word that *describes* sentence *actions*. An adverb tells *where, when,* or *how* something happens. It usually does this by describing the verb in the sentence. An adverb can also describe some other part of speech. See **2c-2e**.

These adverbs tell *where* the action happens.

They met *downtown*.

There they are.

These adverbs tell *when* the action happens.

He arrived *late*.

She left *yesterday*.

These adverbs tell *how* the action happens.

She slept *poorly*.

The wolf *slowly* chewed on the bones.

Agreement The forms of words that show the same number. See **Chapter 7.**

One *tap means* to be quiet.

Two *taps mean* you can speak.

When you hear *three taps, they* mean you should shout.

Antecedent The word or group of words referred to by a following pronoun.

The *person who* leaves last can turn out the light.

Antonym A word that means the opposite of another word.

up/down, high/low, hot/cold, sad/happy

Apostrophe A mark that looks like a comma above the line to show possession, missing letters, or the plural of numbers. See **11e (1)-(3); 11f.**

Ma's hat, can't, 4's.

Appositive A word or group of words placed next to another to explain a meaning or idea.

> She raced in the motocross, *a sort of cross-country motorcycle race.*
> Jennie, *the leader,* hit a bump on the last turn.

Article The words *a, an,* and *the.* An article is a kind of adjective. See **1g.**

Auxiliary verb (See **Helping verb.**)

Case The form of a pronoun that shows its relation to other parts of the sentence.

> SUBJECTIVE CASE usually serves as the subject of a sentence.

> *He* sleeps.

> POSSESSIVE CASE shows ownership.

> *His* dog is sleeping.

> OBJECTIVE CASE usually serves as the object of the sentence or the object of a preposition.

> Don't wake *him.*
> Give the bone to *her.*

Clause A group of words with both a subject and a predicate. A clause can be a sentence or part of a sentence.

> INDEPENDENT CLAUSE A clause that can stand alone as a complete thought.

> *The wind blew* and *the branch broke.* [two clauses in one sentence]
> *The wind blew. The branch broke.* [separate sentences]

DEPENDENT CLAUSE A clause that depends upon an independent clause to complete its thought.

When the wind blew, the branch broke.

A dependent clause can work like a noun, an adjective, or an adverb in a sentence.

Colloquial Acceptable words or forms in informal conversation, but usually not acceptable in formal speech or writing.

Take it easy.
Stay cool.

Comparison The forms of an adjective or adverb that show more or less about the words they describe. (See also **Modifiers**.) See **1h; 2d.**

POSITIVE *mad, good*
COMPARATIVE *madder, better*
SUPERLATIVE *maddest, best*

Completer A word or words that complete a statement about the subject of a sentence. A completer comes after the verb. It is part of the predicate. (See also **Predicate**.) See **4e-4f.**

Completers are words or phrases that can fit in sentence blanks like these:

Jim kicked _____ .
He hurt _____ .
You are _____ .

NOUNS AND NOUN WORD GROUP COMPLETERS
Jim kicked *the door.*
He hurt *his big toe.*
You are *the captain.*

ADJECTIVE COMPLETER
You are *old*.

ADVERB COMPLETER
You are *there*.

Complex sentence   A sentence with an independent clause and a dependent clause. (See also **Clause.**)

> I feel angry whenever he comes in. [*I feel angry* is the independent clause; *whenever he comes in* is the dependent clause.]

Compound   A word or group of words made up of two or more parts that could stand alone. See **4b (3)-(4); 4c.**

> COMPOUND WORD *chairperson, basketball*
> COMPOUND SUBJECT *Boys* and *girls* may enter the races.
> COMPOUND OBJECT You may enter the egg *race* and the *relays*.
> COMPOUND PREDICATE Baboons *travel together* and *attack enemies*.

Compound sentence   A sentence made up of two or more independent clauses.

> Abner Beanbag has a skateboard, but he can't stay on it.

Compound verb   Two or more verbs in a clause or sentence.

> Yolanda Faraday *picked* and *ate* all the berries.

Conjunction   A word that connects words, phrases, or clauses. The two kinds of conjunctions are *coordinating conjunctions* and *subordinating conjunctions*. See **2g**.

COORDINATING CONJUNCTIONS connect parts of words, phrases, or clauses. The most common coordinating conjunctions are *and, but,* and *or.*

bread *and* butter
peace *but* not freedom
over the hills *and* through the valleys
She goes *or* you die!

SUBORDINATING CONJUNCTIONS connect ideas not equal to each other. Some examples are *after, although, as, because, before, like, since, though, unless, until, when, where, while.*

Terry stayed home *until* the bus came.
I changed the tire *because* it was flat.

Consonants   All alphabet letters that are not vowels (**b, c, d,** for example). Consonant sounds are made in speaking by closing or bringing together parts of the throat, mouth, teeth, tongue, or lips.

Contractions   A word form using an apostrophe to show missing letters.

can't, don't, could've

Dangling modifier   A modifying word or word group without a subject to modify.

Walking toward town, the billboard can be clearly seen. [This sentence seems to say the billboard is walking toward town!]

CORRECTED *Walking toward town,* anyone can clearly see the billboard. [But do not write: Anyone can clearly see the billboard walking toward town.]

Dependent clause   (See **Clause.**)

Determiner   (See also **Article.**) Determiners are words like *a, an, the, one, some, their.* A determiner is a kind of adjective that always is followed by a noun.

a baby, *a* bird, *a* young boy

the tired old man, *an* old car

Determiners help tell whether a noun is singular or plural.

a duck, *two* sparrows, *some* fish

a fish, *eight* dogs, *the* dolphin

Diacritical marks   Marks used with letters to show how they are pronounced.

ā [as in *say*], ĕ [as in *set*], ä [as in *father*]

Diagraming   A way of showing how parts of a sentence relate to one another. Two main types of diagraming are sometimes used. One type is a traditional diagram. The other is a tree diagram.

Any diagram of a sentence is only one way of showing the relationships among parts of a sentence.

TRADITIONAL DIAGRAMING: Six sentences are diagramed below. Each diagram shows how added parts of a sentence fit together.

(1) The spider wove a web.

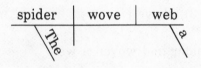

[The simple subject belongs first on the horizontal line. Under it on a slanted line belongs its modifier. The verb follows the simple subject, separated by a vertical line through the horizontal line. The direct object follows the verb, separated by a vertical line resting on the horizontal line.]

(2) The hairy spider wove a web.

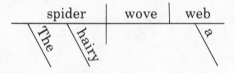

[Additional modifiers of the subject belong on additional slanted lines.]

(3) The hairy spider on the ceiling wove a web.

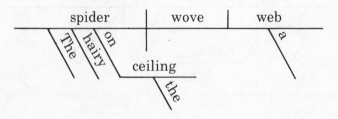

[A prepositional phrase modifying the subject belongs on slanted and horizontal lines as shown in (3), above.]

(4) The spider had woven a web.

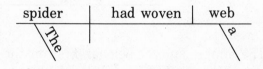

[Helping verbs belong with the main verb on the horizontal line.]

(5) The spider wove a web carefully.

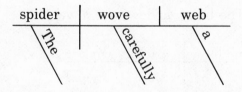

[An adverb belongs on a slanted line under the verb it modifies.]

(6) The hairy spider on the ceiling had woven a large web carefully.

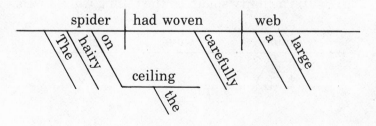

Here are two ways to correct each sentence:

1. I do*n't* have one. (or any) [Remove second negative.]
   I have none. [Remove first negative.]
2. I didn't say a thing. (or anything) [Remove second negative.]
   I said nothing. [Remove the first negative. Change *say* to *said* so it will mean the same thing as *did say.*]

Expletive The word *it* or *there* when used as a filler to start a sentence.

It is going to rain.
There was not a cloud in the sky.

Exposition Writing that expresses, explains, or "exposes" one's ideas, for example, a newspaper editorial, an essay, or a research paper.

Fragment An incomplete sentence, one without either the necessary subject or predicate. See **4g.**

Charging up the hill. [Who or what is charging?]

CORRECTED The wild horses came charging up the hill.

Helping verb Words that are used with verbs. The most common helping verbs are listed here. See **2a(3).**

am, are, is, was, were, being, been
do, does, did, done
have, has, had

Here are some other common helping verbs:

> can, could, may, shall
> will, would, might

Helping verbs help the verb express their actions.

> Jerry *is* trying hard.
> Jim *does* work hard, too.
> She *may* work as long as she wants to.
> I *wouldn't* go.

Helping verbs also help show time.

> I *shall* quit if he stays. [action in the future]
> I *have* eaten the apples. [action completed in the past]

Idiom   A word or phrase used in a special way.

> She *did herself proud.*

Independent clause   A group of words having a subject and a predicate able to stand by itself without need of other words to finish its meaning. (See also **Clause.**)

Indirect object   The secondary receiver of sentence action.

> They gave *him* the booby prize. [To whom did they give the booby prize? Answer: *him*]

Infinitive   The standard or base form of a verb, often with *to*. See **2b(1)**.

> to live, to eat

The infinitive is sometimes used as a noun.

> To sleep is a necessity.

Inflection   The change in the form of a word to show a change in meaning or grammatical use.

> *dog* [singular], *dogs* [plural], *dogs'* [plural possessive]
> *sing* [present], *sang* [past], *sung* [part participle]

Interjection   A part of speech showing strong feeling. An interjection is not grammatically related to the sentence. See **2h.**

> *Shucks!* is all she could say.

Irregular verb   A verb that does not add **ed** to form the past tense. (See also **Verb.**) See **2b(2).**

Italics   Slanted letters printed to draw special attention.

Linking verb   A verb that links the subject to the subject completer. See **2a(2).**

> *appear, become, feel, look,* and forms of the verb *be.*

Main Clause   An independent clause.

Metaphor   A figure of speech in which one item is compared to another.

> The cloud was *a puff of cotton.*

Modal auxiliary A verb used as a verb helper that does not change form.

can, could, might, ought

Modifiers Words describing someone, something, or some action. (See also **Adjective** and **Adverb**.)

Mood The purpose of the speaker as shown in the form and use of the verb. The three moods are (1) to state something, (2) to order or request something, and (3) to show a condition that is not true or is desirable.

(1) INDICATIVE MOOD She *has* a new bicycle.
(2) IMPERATIVE MOOD *Move* over, please.
(3) SUBJUNCTIVE MOOD We wish you *were* here.

Nominative The subjective case. (See also **Case**.)

Nonrestrictive clause or phrase A group of words that tells something more about someone or something in the same sentence. A nonrestrictive clause or phrase is not necessary to make the sentence complete, but it adds to its meaning.

The ancient car, *rusted and dented,* sat behind the garage. [phrase]
The ancient car, *which was rusted and dented from years of misuse,* sat behind the garage. [clause]

Noun A noun names a *person, place, thing,* or *idea.* See **1a.**

Names of persons: Luis Ortiz, Barbara Allen, Cheri Baba [proper nouns]
Names of places: Jones Alley, New York City, Mars [proper nouns]
Names of things: clouds, houses, horses [common nouns]
Names of ideas: love, hope, freedom [common nouns]

Number   One or more than one person or thing. In English, singular or plural number is shown in most nouns by the addition of **s** or **es.** See **7a.**

goat/goat**s**, match/match**es**

A few nouns change their spellings in special ways.

woman/women, ox/oxen, goose/geese

Number is shown in most pronouns by a change in form.

this/these, that/those, he, she/they, her, him/them, hers, his/theirs

Object   The result of action or the receiver of the action in a sentence. See **4e.**

DIRECT OBJECT She loves her *dog.*
INDIRECT OBJECT They gave *him* the money.

The object of a preposition is a noun or pronoun which is related to another word by the preposition. See pp. 45–46.

Give the spade to *him.*

Objective case   Pronouns show the objective case when they serve as the objects of a sentence or of a preposition. (See also **Case**.)

> Tom introduced *him* to *her*. [*Him* and *her* are in the objective case.]

Paragraph   A paragraph is a group of sentences beginning with an indention. The sentences should all be about one idea. There should be enough sentences to make the idea clear to the reader. See **5a**.

The topic of a paragraph is often written in a topic sentence. The topic sentence usually comes at the beginning of a paragraph. See **5b**.

> *She always did nice things for her little brother.* She always saved any treats she had to share with him. She would even help him to do his chores. She'd read him stories at bedtime. And she'd walk him anywhere he was too young to go by himself.

Participle   The **ing** or the **ed** form of a verb that can be used as an adjective. A few irregular verbs form their participles in irregular ways. (See also **Phrase**.)

> happening [present participle]
> happened [past participle]
> broken [past participle of irregular *break*]

Parts of speech   English sentences can have eight main kinds of words in them. These eight kinds of words are called parts of speech. These words do the work of the sentence. They help show meaning.

The eight parts of speech are *noun, pronoun, verb, adjective, adverb, preposition, conjunction,* and *interjection.* (See separate listings.)

Phrase   A group of words belonging together, but not making a complete statement. See **3a-3c.**

> PREPOSITIONAL PHRASE *into the house*
> VERB PHRASE *having eaten*
> NOUN PHRASE *a wonderful meal*

Plural   More than one. The plural is shown by words that mean more than one (*many, ten*). It is also shown in the forms of nouns (*man/men*), pronouns (*her/them*), and verbs (she *runs*/they *run*).

Possessive   A form of a noun or pronoun showing that someone owns something or that things belong close together.

> the *girl's* purse [possessive noun]
> *his* idea [possessive pronoun]

Predicate   The part of a sentence that tells about the subject. See **4b(2).**

> S   P
> The bobcat *grabbed the meat and ran up the tree.*

> PREDICATE ADJECTIVE (See **Completer.**)
> PREDICATE NOUN (See **Completer.**)

Prefix   A prefix is one or more syllables added to the front of a word or root to affect its meaning. See **13b(9).**

unhappy, preview, repay, underline, disturb, subway, copilot, indirect, nonpayment

Preposition   A part of speech that points out how two words are related. Most prepositions show time or place or direction. See **2f.**

in a minute, *of* the tree, *before* the meeting

Prepositional phrase   (See **Phrase.**)

Pronoun   A word that can stand for a noun. Usually, a pronoun stands for a group of words in which the noun is the main word. See **1d.**

The shy young boy walked into the room. *He* walked into the room. [*He* stands for the group of words.]

The wolf with the broken paw snarled at Tom. *It* snarled at him.

That is *Jane's* ball.
That is *her* ball.

Three cases of pronouns are found above. The first is the *subjective case.* It usually shows the doer of the action in a sentence.

He walked into the room.
It snarled at him.

The second case of the pronoun is the *objective case.*

It snarled at *him.*

The third case of a pronoun is the *possessive case.*

That is *her* ball.
We're going to Terri and Sally's house. We're going to *their* house.

Punctuation The marks used with words to show how they relate and how they are to be read. See **Chapter 10.**

Root The basic part of a word. Parts are added to it to change its meaning. (See also **Prefix** and **Suffix.**) See **13b(9).**

> dis*turb*, re*play*, *play*able

Run-on sentence Two or more sentences run together without correct punctuation or connecting words. See **4h.**

> Some fishermen cast out lines and hauled in fish others packed the fish in ice.

> CORRECTED Some fishermen cast out lines and hauled in fish. Others packed the fish in ice.

Sentence A group of related words needing no other words to complete its thought. A sentence has a *subject* and a *predicate*. See **4a** and **4b.**

> SENTENCE The paper was crumpled and torn.
> NONSENTENCE Crumpled and torn paper. (See also **Fragment.**)

Singular Only one of anything. (See **Plural** for a comparison.)

Slang A word or phrase not yet accepted for general use by most educated people.

> That's a *tough break.*
> See that *jazzy* pair of shoes.

Subject   A noun (or its equal) that the rest of its sentence says or asks something about. The subject of a sentence is the *who* or *what* that belongs with the predicate. See **4b(1)**.

> *Vic* played basketball.
> *Africa* is a huge continent.

Subject completer   (See **Completer**.)

Subordinate clause   A dependent clause. (See also **Clause**.)

Subordinating conjunction   (See **Conjunction**.)

Suffix   One or more syllables that add meaning to a word or root. A suffix is added to the end of a word or a root. See **13b(10)**.

> retire*ment*, slow*ly*, fast*er*, short*est*, fool*ish*, play*fully*, six*th*, flex*ible*

Syllable   A letter or group of letters containing a vowel that is pronounced as one unit. A syllable may be a single vowel.

> i-so-late, e-ject, a-ble

Most syllables contain a vowel sound plus a consonant sound or sounds.

> re-mind, re-veal, se-cret (2 syllables)
> con-struc-tion, in-sur-ance, re-place-ment (3 syllables)
> in-tro-duc-tion, re-place-a-ble (4 syllables)

Synonym   A word that means the same as another.

> fast/quick   tired/weary   old/aged

Syntax   The arrangement of words and parts of a sentence.

> The class awarded her the trophy.
> The class awarded the trophy to her.
> She was awarded the trophy by the class.

Tense   Time as shown by the form of a verb. See **2b.**

> PRESENT you *watch,* he *watches*
>
> PAST you *watched,* she *watched*
>
> FUTURE you *will watch,* they *are going to watch*

Topic sentence   (See **Paragraph.**)

Transformation   The changes in form that can be made in sentences and word groups.

Unity   In composition, making sentences refer to the same topic or subject.

Verb   A part of speech that shows action (*run*), states something (*is*), or shows condition (*seems*). Most verbs change their form to show time (*run–ran*). (See **Tense.**) Other changes show number (One woman *was* there. More *were* not.) See **2a.**

A verb tells the action in a sentence. Or it tells that something exists. *Exists* means "is" or "to be."

> *action:* runs, yells, sleeps
> *exists:* is, are, am, was, were

Verbal   A form of a verb used as another part of speech. (See **Infinitive**.)

Vocabulary   The words and their meanings used in a language.

Voice   The form of a verb that shows who or what is doing something.

> ACTIVE VOICE A bee stung her.
> PASSIVE VOICE She was stung by a bee.

Vowel   The letters **a, e, i, o u,** and sometimes the letters **y** and **w.**

INDEX

TAB KEY INDEX

Tab Key Index
(continued)

CORRECTION SYMBOL	DEFINITION	CHAPTER
plan	planning and writing a composition	6
prep	preposition	2
pro	pronoun	1
ref	reference of pronouns	7
ro	run-on sentence	4
sp	spelling	13
spk	speaking and listening	12
ss	sentence structure	4
verb	verb	2
ww	wrong word	8
¶	paragraph	5
.	period	10
?	question mark	10
!	exclamation mark	10
,	comma	10
;	semicolon	
:	colon	11
-	hyphen	11
"	quotation marks	11
( )	parentheses	

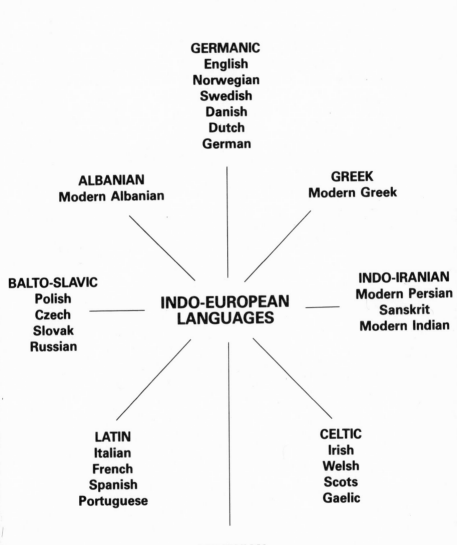